THE ROYAL COURT THEA

Scenes from a Repatriation

By Joel Tan

Scenes from a Repatriation was first performed at the Royal Court Jerwood Theatre Upstairs on Friday 25 April 2025.

Scenes from a Repatriation
By Joel Tan

Cast (in alphabetical order):

Kaja Chan
Aidan Cheng
Jon Chew
Fiona Hampton
Robin Khor Yong Kuan
Sky Yang

Director **emma + pj**
Designer **TK Hay**
Lighting Designer **Alex Fernandes**
Sound Designer & Composer **Patch Middleton**
Video Designer **Tyler Forward**
Casting Director **Jatinder Chera**
Movement Director **Ken Nakajima**
Dialect & Language **Jenru Wang**
Assistant Designer **Yijing Chen**
Production Manager **Zara Drohan**
Costume Supervisor **Ellen Rey de Castro**
Company Manager **Mica Taylor**
Stage Manager **Aime Neeme**
Deputy Stage Manager **Daze Corder**
Lighting Supervisor **Lucinda Plummer**
Lighting Programmer **Philip Burke**
Lead Producer **Hannah Lyall**
Executive Producer **Steven Atkinson**

emma + pj would like to thank Nicola T. Chang, Jemima Yong, Angela Wai Nok Hui, Jen Leong, Bonnie Chan, Isis Clunie, Mascuud Dahir, Chusi Amoros, Joe Boylan, Will Spence, Rosa Garland, Paula Varjack, Stella Green and The London Lion Dance.

The Royal Court wish to thank the following for their help
with this production: Ellison Tan Yuyang and Wahwah Hung Chit-wah.

Joel Tan (Writer)

As writer, for the Royal Court: **Living Newspaper.**

As writer, other theatre includes: **G*d is a Woman (Wild Rice, Singapore); No Particular Order (Theatre503); Tartuffe (Wild Rice, Singapore); When The Daffodils (Orange Tree); Overheard (Chinese Arts Now); My White Best Friend (and Other Letters Left Unsaid), (Bunker); Tango (Pangdemonium, Singapore); Café (Twenty Something Theatre Festival, Singapore); Mosaic (Singtel Waterfront Theatre, Singapore); The Way We Go (Checkpoint Theatre, Singapore).**

As dramaturg, theatre includes: **You are Here (Wild Rice, Singapore).**

emma + pj (Director)

emma + pj is the collaboration between theatre makers Emma Clark and PJ Stanley. They were previously artists in residence at the Barbican Centre and The Spring Arts and Heritage Centre and lead facilitators for Yardlings at The Yard Theatre.

Theatre includes: **Ghosts of the Near Future (Barbican/UK Tour); The Shivers (New Diorama/UK Tour); Atlantic (VAULT Festival).**

Kaja Chan (Performer)

Theatre includes: **The 47th (Old Vic).**

Television includes: **Absentia, Bridgerton, 1899.**

Film includes: **Anniversary, Flight 298.**

Yijing Chen (Assistant Designer)

Theatre includes: **Thunderstorm (ADC); We're Few and Far Between (White Bear & Drayton Arms).**

Awards include: **The Linbury Prize for Stage Design.**

Aidan Cheng (Performer)

Theatre includes: **The Good Person of Szechwan (Sheffield Crucible/Lyric Hammersmith); The King of Hell's Palace (Hampstead); Macbeth (Globe).**

Television includes: **3 Body Problem, You, Red Eye, Sky's Devils, The Girlfriend Experience, Harlots.**

Jatinder Chera (Casting Director)

For the Royal Court: **G.**

Other theatre includes: **Lavender, Hyacinth, Violet, Yew, The Real Ones, A Playlist For The Revolution, Sleepova, The P Word (The Bush); Marriage Material (Lyric Hammersmith); The Comeuppance (Almeida); Sweat (Royal Exchange); Multiple Casualty Incident, Samuel Takes A Break, The Flea (The Yard).**

Awards include: **Olivier award for outstanding achievement in an affiliate theatre (Sleepova), Olivier award for outstanding achievement in an affiliate theatre (The P Word).**

Jon Chew (Performer)

Theatre includes: **Pacific Overtures (Menier Chocolate Factory); The Good Person of Szechwan (Sheffield Crucible/Lyric Hammersmith); Anything Goes (Barbican); The King and I (London Palladium); Forgotten Chinese Characters (Arcola); Wild Goose Dreams (Theatre Royal, Bath); Asian Pirate Musical (Vaults Festival); Unity 1918, Cock (The Actor's Studio); Angels in America Part 1 (Damansara Performing Arts Centre); The Bee, Philadelphia Here I Come!, The Last Five Years, Birdy, Boom (Kuala Lumpur Performing Arts Centre).**

Television includes: **Silo, The Great, KAOS, EastEnders, Doctors, The First Team, Nova Jones.**

Film includes: **Robin and the Hood.**

Radio includes: **Curse of the Five Elements: Fire, Dragons of the Pool, A Many-Splendoured Thing, The Good Earth, Zoetrope.**

Daze Corder (Deputy Stage Manager)

Theatre includes: **52 Monologues for Young Transsexuals, Ugly Sisters (piss / CARNATION); The Ballad of Hattie and James, The Purists (Kiln); Everything I Own (Sankofa Productions & Brixton House); Jobsworth (Prentice Productions).**

Alex Fernandes (Lighting Designer)

Theatre includes: **Domestica, Swimming Pools (Sleepwalk Collective); Double Double Act (Made In China); The Talent (Action Hero); Two Billion Beats (Orange Tree); Paradise Now! (Bush); Heartbreaking Final (Tim Etchells); l'Addition (Festival International d'Avignon); A View from the Bridge (Headlong); The Beginning (Bert & Nasi); Ghosts of the Near Future (emma + pj); Black Sheep (Curious Directive); Die Glasmenagerie (Theater Basel).**

Dance includes: **Système AI (Sadler's Wells); Minor Planets (HAU Berlin); Kim Kardashian (Balé da Cidade de Palmas).**

Awards include: **Michael Northen Bursary 2013 (ALPD).**

Tyler Forward (Video Designer)

For the Royal Court: **The Legends of Them, G.**

As designer, theatre includes: **Spitfire Girls (Tour); Death on the Throne The Loosical (Upstairs at the Gatehouse); The 25th Annual Putnam County Spelling Bee, A Midsummer Night's Dream, Sunday in the Park with George (Mack); The Turn of The Screw (Queens); Dorian The Musical (Southwark Playhouse); Redcliffe (Turbine); Diana The Musical Concert (Eventim Apollo); Trompe L'Oiel (The Other Palace); Loserville (Blackheath Halls); Our House (Albany); No Man's Island, Redemption, Mission (The Big House); Play, The Games (P&O Arvia); Silence (Donmar/Tara); Musical Theatre Showcase (Trinity Laban); Roles We'll Never Play, Close Quarters (RADA); Opening Up: The Mental Health Musical (Union); Thoroughly Modern Millie (Electric); Nor Woman Neither (Tristan Bates); Macbeth (Vanbrugh); Stoning Mary (George Bernard Shaw).**

As designer, exhibitions include: **Wes Anderson's Asteroid City, Future Shock.** As associate designer, theatre includes: **Oscar at The Crown (Immersive Show); Belle Livingstone's 58th Street Country Club, Burlesque The Musical (UK Premiere); Carlos Acosta's Nutcracker, Once The Musical Concert, Spongebob The Musical (Tour); Umm Kulthum & The Goldern Era (Bahrain National & Ithra); King Lear (West End); The House With Chicken Legs (Tour); The Trials (Marlowe).**

As associate designer, exhibitions include: **Wes Anderson's French Dispatch.**

TK Hay (Designer)

Theatre includes: **Pea and The Princess (Polka); The Jungle Book (Theatre by the Lake); My Father's Fable (Bush); Little Shop of Horrors (Octagon Bolton, Ipswich New Wolsey, Theatre by the Lake, Hull Truck); Brenda's Got a Baby (New Diorama); G*d is a Woman (Wild Rice); Mosaic (Esplanade); Re:Assembly, Assembly (Drama Box); Mayflies (York Royal); We Will Be Who We Are (Vault Festival); Beginning (Royal Exchange); The Making of a Monster (Wales Millenium Centre); Constellations (Stephen Joseph); The Apology, Tsunagu/Connect (New Earth); An Adventure (Octagon Bolton); The Good, The Bad and The Sholay (Checkpoint); Karius and Baktus (Norwegian Cultural Centre).**

Opera includes: **Alcina (The Opera People).**

Awards include: **The Arts Foundation Fellowship for Theatre, The Stage Debut Awards for Best Designer, The Linbury Prize for Stage Design.**

Fiona Hampton (Performer)

Theatre includes: **The Forsyte Sage (Park Theatre); Touching the Void (Bristol Old Vic/West End); Metamorphoses, Ralegh: The Treason Trail, Much Ado About Nothing (Globe); Tamburlaine (New Earth Theatre); A Midsummer's Dream (New Wolsey Theatre); The Glass Menagerie, Tull, Of Mice and Men, Lighthearted Intercourse, Private Lives, Winter Hill (Octagon); Playhouse Creatures (Chichester Festival); The Changeling (Southwark Playhouse); The Merchant of Venice (Derby Playhouse).**

Television includes: **Nutriciously Nicola, Summer Lane Drive, The Collection, Switch, Holby City and The Sarah Jane Adventures.**

Film includes: **The Good Neighbour; The Windmill; Kingsman: Secret Service.**

Robin Khor Yong Kuan (Performer)

Theatre includes: **Bat Night Market (LIFT); Imperial Troopers (Blaagaard Theatre, Copenhagen), The Magic Flute (Festival d'Aix-en-Provence); Moon Rabbit (Lakeside Arts Nottingham); Strange Tales (Traverse); Let Me Play The Lion Too (Barbican).**

Television includes: **Mind Game, Daddy Dearest, The Precedents.**

Film includes: **High Wire, Rain Town.**

Patch Middleton
(Sound Designer & Composer)

Theatre includes: **Ghosts of the Near Future (Summerhall & Barbican); The Shivers (London Schools Tour); The Mosinee Project (Underbelly & New Diorama); Radiant Boy (Southwark Playhouse).**

Ken Nakajima (Movement Director)

For the Royal Court: **Word-Play.**

Theatre includes: **Seeking Shadows (Rich Mix); A Shanty for an Atomic Town (Obscura Theatre); I'm Going Away Now (Teatro Capodistria); Guidelines (Camden People's Theatre); Pore (Colour Factory).**

Film includes: **OKLOU (NTS Radio); Godspeed (Lowswimmer); IRL (Lowswimmer); GOT GAME? (Jaded London); Accelerate (Yiling Zhao); I Am Your Daughter (Florence Rose); Johanna Parv SS24 (London Fashion Week); SIRPLUS SS23, MACHINE-A SS23.**

Aime Neeme (Stage Manager)

For the Royal Court: **Gunter (& Dirty Hare), Bullring Techno Makeout Jamz (& Ellie Keel Productions).**

Other theatre includes: **Bellringers (& Atticist), An Interrogation (Ellie Keel Productions); Nation (YESYESNONO); Hungry, Black Love, May Queen, Really Big and Really Loud (Paines Plough); How to Save the Planet When You're a Young Carer and Broke, Parakeet (Boundless).**

Ellen Rey de Castro
(Costume Supervisor)

Theatre includes: **The Jungle Book (Theatre By The Lake); My Father's Fable (Bush); The Cardinal (Southwark Playhouse).**

Dance includes: **Sleeping Beauty (Royal Ballet).**

Opera includes: **Lady Macbeth of Mtsensk, Simon Boccanegra (Royal Opera House).**

Jenru Wang (Dialect & Language)

Theatre includes: **My Neighbour Totoro (Barbican & Gillian Lynne), Worth (Arcola & Storyhouse).**

Television includes: **The Agency, Young Sherlock, A Thousand Blows, The Lazarus Project, Devils Series 2, Hanna Series 2.**

Film includes: **The Fantastic Four: First Steps.**

Games include: **Age of Empire: The Three Kingdoms; Assassin's Creed: Codename Jade.**

Voice Over includes: **Walking with Dinosaurs – The Arena Spectacular (Global Creatures in association with BBC Earth).**

Sky Yang (Performer)

Theatre includes: **The Book of Dust (Bridge).**

Television includes: **Halo Series 1, Holding.**

Film includes: **Rebel Moon, Shoulders, Anniversary, Last Days, Whistle, Tomb Raider.**

THE ROYAL COURT THEATRE

The Royal Court Theatre is the writers' theatre. It is a leading force in world theatre for cultivating and supporting writers - undiscovered, emerging and established.

Since 1956, we have commissioned and produced hundreds of writers, from John Osborne to Mohamed-Zain Dada. Royal Court plays from every decade are now performed on stages and taught in classrooms and universities across the globe.

Through the writers, the Royal Court is at the forefront of creating restless, alert, provocative theatre about now. We open our doors to the unheard voices and free thinkers that, through their writing, change our way of seeing.

We strive to create an environment in which differing voices and opinions can co-exist. In current times, it is becoming increasingly difficult for writers to write what they want or need to write without fear, and we will do everything we can to rise above a narrowing of viewpoints.

Through all our work, we strive to inspire audiences and influence future writers with radical thinking and provocative discussion.

royalcourt royalcourttheatre

Supported using public funding by
ARTS COUNCIL ENGLAND

ROYAL COURT SUPPORTERS

Our incredible community of supporters makes it possible for us to achieve our mission of nurturing and platforming writers at every stage of their careers. Our supporters are part of our essential fabric – they help to give us the freedom to take bigger and bolder risks in our work, develop and empower new voices, and create world-class theatre that challenges and disrupts the theatre ecology.

To all our supporters, thank you. You help us to write the future.

PUBLIC FUNDING

Supported using public funding by
ARTS COUNCIL ENGLAND

CHARITABLE PARTNERS

The Common Humanity Arts Trust

BackstageTrust

COCKAYNE

JERWOOD FOUNDATION

CORPORATE SPONSORS & SUPPORTERS
Aqua Financial Ltd
Cadogan
Concord Theatricals
Edwardian Hotels, London
NJA Ltd. – Core Values & Creative Management
Nick Hern Books
Phone Locker
Riverstone Living
Sustainable Wine Solutions
Walpole

CORPORATE MEMBERS
Bloomberg Philanthopies
Sloane Stanley

PRESS NIGHT PARTNER
Prime Time

SISTER

TRUSTS & FOUNDATIONS

Bruce Wake Charitable Trust
Chalk Cliff Trust
Clare McIntyre's Bursary
Cowley Charitable Foundation
The Davidson PlayGC Bursary
The Fenton Arts Trust
Foyle Foundation
Garrick Charitable Trust
The Golsoncott Foundation
John Lyon's Charity
John Thaw Foundation
The Lynne Gagliano Writers' Award
The Marlow Trust
Martin Bowley Charitable Trust
The Noël Coward Foundation
Old Possum's Practical Trust
Richard Radcliffe Charitable Trust
The Royal Borough of Kensington & Chelsea Arts Grant
Rose Foundation
Theatres Trust
The Thompson Family Charitable Trust
The T.S. Eliot Foundation
Unity Theatre Trust
Y.A.C.K F.O

INDIVIDUAL SUPPORTERS

Artistic Director's Circle

Eric Abraham
Katie Bradford
Jeremy & Becky Broome
Clyde Cooper
Debbie De Girolamo &
Ben Babcock
Dominique & Neal Gandhi
Lydia & Manfred Gorvy
David & Jean Grier
Charles Holloway OBE
Linda Keenan
Andrew Rodger and Ariana Neumann
Jack Thorne & Rachel Mason
Sandra Treagus for
ATA Assoc. LTD
Sally Whitehill & Mark Gordon
Anonymous

Writers' Circle

Chris & Alison Cabot
Cas Donald
Robyn Durie
Ellie & Roger Guy
Kater Gordon
The Hon P N Gibson's Charity Trust
Melanie J. Johnson
Nicola Kerr
Héloïse and Duncan
Matthews KC
Emma O'Donoghue
Clare Parsons & Tony Langham
Maureen & Tony Wheeler
Anonymous

Directors' Circle

Piers Butler
Fiona Clements
Professor John Collinge
Julian & Ana Garel-Jones
Carol Hall
Dr Timothy Hyde

Platinum Circle

Moira Andreae
Katie Bullivant
Anthony Burton CBE
Matthew Dean
Emily Fletcher
Beverley Gee
Damien Hyland
Roderick & Elizabeth Jack
Susanne Kapoor
David P Kaskel &
Christopher A Teano
Peter & Maria Kellner
Robert Ledger &
Sally Moulsdale
Frances Lynn
Mrs Janet Martin
Andrew McIver
Brian & Meredith Niles
Corinne Rooney
Anita Scott
Bhags Sharma
Dr Wendy Sigle
Rita Skinner
Brian Smith
Mrs Caroline Thomas
Ian, Victoria & Lucinda Watson
Sir Robert & Lady Wilson
Beverley Buckingham
The Edwin Fox Foundation
Lucy and Spencer De Grey
Madeleine Hodgkin
Barbara Minto
Timothy Prager
Sir Paul & Lady Ruddock
James and Victoria Tanner
Yannis Vasatis
Anonymous

With thanks to our Silver and Gold Supporters, and our Friends and Good Friends, whose support we greatly appreciate.

Royal Court Theatre
Sloane Square,
London SW1W 8AS
Tel: 020 7565 5050
info@royalcourttheatre.com
www.royalcourttheatre.com

Artistic Director
David Byrne
Executive Director
Will Young
Artistic Director's Office Manager
Natalie Dodd

Senior Associate Playwright & Dramaturg
Gillian Greer
Associate Playwright & Young Writers' Associate
Beth Flintoff
Associate Playwrights
**Mike Bartlett,
Ryan Calais Cameron,
Vinay Patel, Ishy Din,
Nina Segal.**
Associate Artist (Art Direction)
Guy J Sanders
New Plays Associate
Laetitia Somé
Resident Director
Aneesha Srinivasan
Artistic Co-ordinator
Ailsa Dann
Playwrights '73 bursary attachment
Tife Kusoro

Head of Producing & Partnerships
Steven Atkinson
Producers
**Hannah Lyall,
Ralph Thompson.**
New Writers & Participation Producer
Tabitha Hayward
Producing Co-ordinator
Winnie Imara

Director of Development
Anuja Batra
Development Officers
**Ellena Sychrava,
Nash Metaxas.**

Head of Production
Marius Rønning
Production Manager
Zara Drohan
Company Manager
Mica Taylor^
Head of Lighting
Deanna Towli
Deputy Head of Lighting
Lucinda Plummer
Lighting Technician
Izzy Hobby
Lighting Programmer
Lizzie Skellett
Head of Stage
Steve Evans
Deputy Head of stage
Maddy Collins
Stage Show Technician
Oscar Sale
Head of Sound
David McSeveney
Deputy Head of Sound
Jet Sharp
Head of Costume
Lucy Walshaw
Deputy Head of Costume
Phoebe Firth

Director of Marketing & Communications
Rachael Welsh
Marketing & Sales Manager
Benjamin McDonald
Digital Content Producer (Videography)
Giovanni Edwards
Marketing Officer
Elizabeth Carpenter
Communications Assistant
Natasha Ryszka-Onions
Press & Publicity
Bread and Butter PR

Finance Director
Helen Perryer
Finance Manager
Olivia Amory
Senior Finance & Payroll Officer
Will Dry
Finance & Administration Assistant
Bukola Sonubi

Head of People
Olivia Shaw
People and Governance Coordinator
Ayushi Mahajan

General Manager
Rachel Dudley
Front of House Manager
Jennelle Reece-Gardner
Box Office Manager
Poppy Templeton
Senior Duty House Manager
Ronay Poole
Ushers/Duty House Managers
**Emer Halton-O'Mahony,
James Wilson.**
Box Office Sales Assistants
**William Byam Shaw,
Ollie Harrington, Aidan Thompson-Coates.**
Box Office & Administration Assistant
Phoebe Coop
Stage Door Keepers
**James Graham,
Léa Jackson,
Paul Lovegrove.**

Head of Operations & Sustainability
Robert Smael
Bar & Kitchen Manager
Adam Turns
Lead Cook
Verity Heath
Senior Bar & Floor Supervisor
Lucy Stepan
Assistant Cooks
Toby Beynon, Oscar Faulkner, Sofia Wills.
Bar & Floor Supervisors
Val Farrow, Matthew Paul, Isa Wood.
General Maintenance Technician
David Brown

Thanks to all of our Ushers and Bar & Kitchen staff.

^ The post of Company Manager is supported by Charles Holloway OBE.

ENGLISH STAGE COMPANY

Honorary Council
**Graham Devlin CBE
Alan Grieve CBE
Martin Paisner CBE
Joyce Hytner OBE
Phyllida Lloyd CBE**

Council Chairman
Anthony Burton CBE

Members
**Jennette Arnold OBE
Noma Dumezweni
Neal Gandhi
Pamela Jikiemi
Mwenya Kawesha
Mark Ravenhill
Andrew Rodger
Anita Scott
Lord Stewart Wood
Mahdi Yahya**

Let's be friends. With benefits.

Our Friends and Good Friends are part of the fabric of the Royal Court. They help us to create world-class theatre, and in return they receive early access to our shows and a range of exclusive benefits.

Join today and become a part of our community.

Become a Friend (from £40 a year)

Benefits include:
- Priority Booking
- Advanced access to £15 Monday tickets
- 10% Bar & Kitchen discount (including Court in the Square)

Become a Good Friend (from £95 a year)

In addition to the Friend benefits, our Good Friends also receive:

- Five complimentary playtexts for Royal Court productions
- An invitation for two to step behind the scenes of the Royal Court Theatre at a special event

Our Good Friends' membership also includes a voluntary donation.
This extra support goes directly towards supporting our work and future, both on and off stage.

To become a Friend or a Good Friend, or to find out more about the different ways in which you can get involved, visit our website: royalcourttheatre.com/support-us

The English Stage Company at the Royal Court Theatre is a registered charity (No. 231242)

SCENES FROM A REPATRIATION

Joel Tan

Characters

Prologue
GROUP OF PEOPLE, *Chinese*
MAN, *Chinese*
WOMAN, *Chinese*
CHILD, *Chinese*

Part One
1.
WITCH ONE, *female, any age and race*
WITCH TWO, *any gender, any age and race*
GUARDS, *any age and race*
YOUNG SOLDIER, *white*
YOUNG WOMAN, *Chinese*
2.
LIM, *any gender, British Chinese*
CURATOR, *any gender, any race*

3.
PROF, *any gender, white*
STUDENT, *any gender, mainland Chinese*

4.
FIVE MUSEUM CURATORS, *any race, any age*

5–7.
POET, *trans non-binary, British Chinese*
DRAG KING, *gender queer, British Chinese*
CROSS TALK PERFORMER A, *British Chinese*
CROSS TALK PERFORMER B, *British Chinese*
DJ, *British Chinese*
VOICE 1 AND 2, *any race, any age*

CHARACTERS

8.
MAN, *white*
WOMAN, *Americanised mainland Chinese*

9.
CLEANER, *male, any race*
CONSERVATOR, *any age and race*
YOUNG SOLDIER, *white*
YOUNG WOMAN, *Chinese*
MAN, *Hong Kong Chinese*

Part Two
1.
WOMAN, *mainland Chinese*
MAN, *mainland Chinese*

2.
YOUNG MAN, *mainland Chinese*
WOMAN, *white*
MAN, *mainland Chinese*

3.
FRIEND, *mainland Chinese*
MAN, *mainland Chinese*

4.
YOUNG MAN, *Uighur*
YOUNG WOMAN, *any race*
POLICE

5.
STONEMASON, *Chinese*
MOTHER, *Chinese*

Note

This play surrounds a statue of the Bodhisattva Guanyin in the British Museum.

It should remain on stage throughout, though it may not be literally present in each scene. How the statue is represented is up to the production, but it should be rendered with respect.

The statue is on a plinth or dais. It is a stone statue, humanlike, child-sized or smaller. It is cast in the 'Royal Ease' pose, right leg hitched up, right arm resting on the right knee. The face is smiling, eyes semi-open.

(*Italicized text in parentheses*) are stage/performance directions. (Non-italicized text in parentheses) are to be played but not spoken.

An en dash (–) on a line alone indicates a beat or pause.

A forward slash (/) indicates an interruption by the next line.

Line breaks in the dialogue are suggestions for shifts in thought or intention, and do not indicate breaks in rhythm. In fact, where a line does not end with a period, the next line can come quickly after.

For the first production, Part Two: Scenes 1 and 2 were translated into Chinese. Part Two: Scene 1 was performed in Mandarin and Cantonese, while Part Two: Scene 2 was eventually performed in English. The translations were provided by Ellison Tan (Mandarin) and Hung Chit Wah (Cantonese), with additional Mandarin translations by Yijing Chen and Robin Khor, and additional Cantonese translations by Bonnie Chan. The translations are available to read online at www.nickhernbooks.co.uk/scenes-from-a-repatriation

This text went to press before the end of rehearsals and so may differ slightly from the play as performed.

Prologue

A burning building. Outside, the sound of men yelling.

Inside, a group of people huddle, choking, coughing, as the fire closes in. A MAN *bangs against the door, hits it with a large stick. Hits it and hits it. It will not budge.*

A WOMAN *holds her* CHILD *close.*

WOMAN. I love you.

CHILD. They're not coming.

WOMAN. I love you.

CHILD. The door's stuck.

WOMAN. I love you.

The MAN *turns to look at the rest. The door will not budge.*

The fire swells.

PART ONE: THE UNITED KINGDOM OF GREAT BRITAIN AND NORTHERN IRELAND

1.

The British Museum.

Lights come up on a statue of the Bodhisattva Guanyin, sitting in the 'Royal Ease' pose. Eyes closed, listening, sleeping, or both.

WITCH ONE *has stopped before the statue. Something in it seems to have called to her. She cannot look away. She tries to, maybe even makes to go, but returns. She slowly sits down. Regards the statue.*

WITCH ONE. I love you too.

Silence.

Oh, I...

(*she's caught by a complicated feeling, perhaps wants to cry*)
(*her phone beeps, she looks at it, ignores it*)
(*she looks around. No one*)
(*she opens her sack, takes out a burning bowl, a smudge stick, palo santo or sage or resins, her praxis is messy, but she's got a sixth sense about things*)

Hello?

(*no reply*)
(*she lights her smudge stick, it doesn't catch*)

Fuck.

(*it lights*)

That's better.
Isn't it?

–

–

–

It's alright.
It's time to
You can –

(*she starts coughing*)

Ooph, something heavy here.
You can go, you can move on.

(*she coughs harder*)

WITCH TWO *enters, sees* WITCH ONE *coughing.*

WITCH TWO. Babe, y'alright?
Drink some water.

WITCH ONE. Thanks.

WITCH TWO. The others are all done, getting some drinks.
You coming?

(*sees the smoking bowl*)

Babe you know we can't…

(*looks around, no one*)

The smoke's gonna…

WITCH ONE. I can't stop looking at this one.
These stains.

WITCH TWO. Uh huh.

WITCH ONE. You ever think?
What's in a stain?

WITCH TWO. Oxidation, I s'pose. Exposure.

WITCH ONE. No, man.
Where one thing meets another.
Imprints itself.

WITCH TWO. Yeah.
You sure you okay?

WITCH ONE. What do you reckon this spot here is?
This dark bit.

WITCH TWO. Blood?

WITCH ONE. I dunno. Blood, yeah.
Worse, maybe?
Soot.

–

Soot, yeah.
Fire.

–

Fire.

(*shudders*)

Horrible to think.

WITCH TWO. Yeah.

WITCH ONE. The heat of it.
The –
hopeless…

WITCH TWO. Cold in here.

WITCH ONE. You want to think it's easy y'know?
Surrendering to death.
Wanna think it's a letting go.
But what about fire?
How do you surrender to fire?
No one surrenders to fire.
You writhe in it.
You scream, you feel it
cook you.

WITCH TWO. Fuck.

WITCH ONE. There's no surrender with fire.
Is there?
Horrible to think someone…
Could do that to someone else.
Anyone.
–

When the fuck are we ever gonna stop doing this shit to one another?

WITCH TWO. Let's go, baby.

WITCH ONE. I wanna pray for this one.
One last one. Please?

WITCH TWO. Course.

They pray together.

It gets hazy from the smoking bowl.

Enter GUARD ONE.

GUARD ONE. Excuse me.

WITCH TWO. Fuck.

GUARD ONE. Sorry you can't do that.
 We've been watching you.

WITCH TWO. We're done, we're going.
 Come on.

But WITCH ONE *is unmoving, almost, in a trance.*

GUARD ONE. We closed an eye with the dancing
 and the flowers
 in that other room
 But this smoke stuff, that's

WITCH TWO. Just incense

GUARD ONE. You try'na set off the fire alarm?

WITCH TWO. It's not going to set off the

GUARD ONE. Yeah, no, it'll –
 Carbon monoxide detector.
 Create a whole mess.
 Ruin the art.
 Put it out, please, and you've gotta –

WITCH ONE. Quiet.

Something in her voice spooks GUARD ONE.

GUARD ONE. You're disturbing the other –

WITCH ONE. 'S no one here.

 –

GUARD ONE. Listen I've been watching you lot.
 You can't just –
 I don't want to have to remove you.

 GUARD ONE *moves to* WITCH ONE, *touches her on her shoulder.*

WITCH TWO. Could you please not touch her.
 Could you –

WITCH TWO *takes out a camera and starts filming* GUARD ONE. *Over the following,* WITCH ONE, *rapt in a prayerful position, is gradually galvanised by some spectral power.*

GUARD ONE. Fuck's sake, *could you please* put that –

WITCH TWO. (*to the camera more than anything*)

(*perhaps a crowd has gathered, and this is to them too*)

We're
We're...
We are Islington Witches for Radical Change
And we're here to release the spirits in these objects
These / objects imprisoned here,

GUARD ONE. Guys... Guys...

WITCH TWO. against their will by the British Museum
Which is an institution of colonial violence
/ A repository of colonial violence
An archive of brutality!

GUARD ONE. (*into talkie*) Guys I'm gonna need some help in Hall Six
Guys, come on.
I'm going to have to escort you both out of the premises.

As GUARD ONE *makes to move them.*

WITCH TWO. These objects are prisoners!
The spirits within them are prisoners!
We are only here to say prayers
We are not touching the objects
We are peacefully demonstrating
Peacefully intervening...

(*starts to sing a song*)

We cast these spells and prayers
Words of release and worship

But the smoke alarm goes off.

This catches GUARD ONE, *who was maybe lying about the smoke detector, by surprise.*

GUARD ONE. What the fuck?

Perhaps the sprinklers go off too.
Enter GUARD TWO.

GUARD TWO. What the FUCK?

The stage fills with smoke, water, wind, everything.

GUARD ONE. JESUS FUCKING CHRIST
PUT THAT OUT NOW

Suddenly, WITCH ONE *lets out a low, mournful sound of lament. The scene seems to freeze.*

WITCH ONE. FIRE.
FIRE.
DO YOU SEE
DO YOU HEAR
CAN YOU HEAR
CAN'T YOU HEAR US?
CAN'T YOU
DON'T YOU SEE US
DON'T YOU HEAR
SMELL US
CHOKING
IN HERE
FAT BOILING
UNDER OUR SKIN

At the climax of this speech, dark figures, perhaps spirits, definitely spirits, have closed in around WITCH ONE.

FIRE.
FIRE.

Something snaps. The figures aren't spirits, they're GUARDS.

The GUARDS *restrain the two* WITCHES.

WITCH ONE *has collapsed into a slump. Over the following,* WITCH TWO *wrestles, resists, is dragged off. It's all very awful and ugly.*

WITCH TWO. Let her go!
Don't touch her!
We are peacefully demonstrating
We are calling for the return of
of
HUMAN REMAINS
FUCK'S SAKE
HUMAN REMAINS
STOLEN –
RELIGIOUS OBJECTS
PEOPLE'S
GODS
WHAT THE FUCK IS WRONG WITH YOU PEOPLE?!

We are not resisting!

Fuck the police!

GUARD ONE. We're not police.

WITCH TWO. FUCK THE BRITISH MUSEUM.

The WITCHES *are gone.*
Two GUARDS *remain as the dust settles.*
The alarm blares.

–

–

–

The alarm stops.

GUARD ONE. Finally.
Y'alright?

GUARD TWO. (*shaken*) Jesus.

GUARD ONE. Every week some new freakshow, huh?
(*into talkie*) Yup they've been removed.
Come on.

PART ONE 13

GUARD TWO. Gives me chills, this place.

GUARD ONE. Hey?

GUARD TWO. Proper chills.

GUARD ONE. Oi.

GUARD TWO. Proper fucking chills.

> GUARD TWO *looks at but does not see two* GHOSTS, *standing where the statue is: a* YOUNG SOLDIER, *white, in nineteenth-century military uniform and, clinging, gnawing, on his leg, a* YOUNG WOMAN, *Chinese, in linen samfu.*
>
> *The* YOUNG SOLDIER *lets out a mournful scream.*

2.

DR LIM, *British Chinese, a gutsy William Dalrymple type, appears.*

LIM. *This* statue is, well...
In this expression, this is:
The Bodhisattva Guanyin.
Who hears the cries of all Man.
Who is mercy incarnate.
In this pose, called Royal Ease,
Guanyin sits, arm
draped over the leg, face
drowsy as if about to fall asleep,
about to enter a dream of pure
light...
Neither male, nor female.
Transcending the body.
Song Dynasty.
Twelfth century.
Think about that.
We are communing with so many dead.

–

How do we look at an object like this?
How are we *meant* to see?
Imagine *a temple*
The glow of candles.
Clouds of incense.
Imagine seeing...
how the stone almost absorbs the smoke.
As if Guanyin
inhales your prayers.
Then imagine, out of the smoke,
this *face,* slowly appearing...
this *face*
that *smile,*
the reassurance of it.
It *knows* when it says:
Everything will be alright.
Imagine being...
that close to
pure, divine, ecstasy.

So my first thought is:

why the fuck
is it overlooking the gift shop?

A snap.

Projection: 'GIANT ASCENDING: ONE THOUSAND YEARS OF CHINESE ART AT THE BRITISH MUSEUM.'

CURATOR. (*uncomfortable laugh*) Well...

It's an 'In Conversation With: Dr Amber Lim [Anthony Lim if male], Department of Chinese Antiquities, School of Oriental and African Studies'. LIM *is sitting on stage with* CURATOR, *who's facilitating this talk.*

LIM. That wasn't a rhetorical / question –

CURATOR. Oh.

(*laughs*)

I wouldn't say it's *overlooking* the...

LIM. Best view in the house.

CURATOR. Sure.
But please, you were talking so stirringly
about the statue's *context*.

LIM. Okay, its context...

CURATOR. Great.

LIM. Its *current context*
Is that it's overlooking the gift shop.

CURATOR. (*laughs*)

LIM. One of mankind's oldest
most profound dreams of
oceanic
motherly mercy.
Chucked.
Like some spare iPhone charger
at the bottom of your drawer.

CURATOR. Now as much as we love your famous
digressions –

LIM. I think most Chinese people growing up in this country,
can relate to that precise
bottom-of-the-drawer feeling.
That's all I ever think about when I look at her.
Have done, ever since I first came here as a kid.
So when I saw that video with those two witches...

CURATOR. Let's get back to / the uh, the

LIM. And there she was, right in the middle / of it all.

CURATOR. to the art!

LIM. Almost like she wanted us to...

CURATOR. The *art*, / Dr Lim.

LIM. to look a little deeper, look a little more –

CURATOR. My friend, we're short on time, so maybe
let's dwell a little bit, on the workmanship,

which earlier you've given me cause to believe is rather special.

–

LIM. Chinese records really only describe
a handful of such castings,
especially in stone, not wood,
which is customary.
This stone was harvested from seaside cliffs.
Most of these stone Guanyins
Would've been famous.
They lived in palaces.
In the most sacred temples.

CURATOR. That's gorgeous.

LIM. So I guess the question I'm skirting around

CURATOR. Yes

LIM. Is how the hell did she get here?

CURATOR. Well, on the plinth here, we'll see it says
'Made out as a gift
To the Museum in 1917
By CT Loo'

LIM. I know. And that's literally all the Museum has on it.

CURATOR. (*laughs*) This was 1917, the bookkeeping was
a fair bit more... laissez-faire back then, let's say,
though CT Loo of course was a major dealer of Chinese antiquities,
to whom we owe the survival of / several works of –

LIM. The man was practically a grave-robber.
With men like that
the paper trail always turns up something disturbing.
If you choose to look,
which ostensibly this museum never did.

CURATOR. (*surprised laugh*)

LIM. See the good thing about Loo is he kept
meticulous receipts
in an archive in Paris.
I went. And I dug.
Took days but I found his logbook.
Inside a rusted box,
thick with almost a hundred years of dust.
Handwritten records,
all in Chinese, of course,
which is maybe why none of this stuff has ever (surfaced)...

CURATOR. Stuff like

LIM. For example, that Loo buys this statue in 1910,
from a Scottish guy called Charles Baker.
In his old age, Baker ran an Irish pub in Shanghai.

LIM flashes a photo on the screen, a black-and-white shot of the statue. It's sitting on a mantle in an old-timey Irish pub surrounded by casks, bottles, and other pub paraphernalia.

CURATOR. My god.

LIM. Before Shanghai, Baker had spent
the last decades of the nineteenth century in Hong Kong.
Now, what business could a man like Baker have had there?

–

CURATOR. Was he a merchant?

LIM. But where would he have
acquired this exceedingly rare
twelfth-century devotional object?

CURATOR. Pirates.
You might as well just (tell us) –

LIM. Baker was a soldier.
based at the first British Garrison in Hong Kong.
Before that, he'd been a rifleman with the
British Infantry in the 1850s.

–

18   SCENES FROM A REPATRIATION

CURATOR. Which regiment?

LIM. Third.

CURATOR. ...

LIM. Which of course we know
   had been deployed to China
   during the Second Opium War.
   What's crucial is that the Third British Infantry
   as we know,
   had marched on Yuanmingyuan
   the Old Summer Palace, in Beijing,
   one of the great palaces of the nineteenth century.
   Baker was there when they burnt the palace down
   Baker was there when the soldiers looted it dry.
   You catch my drift.

   –

   –

CURATOR. That would certainly be a
   concerning addition
   to the object's provenance, if true.
   Though of course,
   to our knowledge nothing places the statue
   at the Old Summer Palace.
   So, delicious as this all is,
   it's conjecture / at (best)

LIM. Well if you let me (finish) –

CURATOR. And we should wrap up.
   I must insist.

LIM. But I –

CURATOR. This is neither the time nor the place,
   and these things typically require
   rigorous fact-finding and –

LIM. All this took me a few weeks / give or take

CURATOR. Exactly!
Exactly.
Sensationalist, gotcha-history,
and I have to say this sort of stunt
is so far beneath someone of your...

–

Sorry, I...
(*aside*) Amber[/Anthony], could we please...

LIM....

–

Actually a few sources do place a statue of this make at Yuanmingyuan.

Another image on the slideshow, a letter.

This one is my favourite.
It's an account by the Old Summer Palace chief of gardens,
in
1751,
it describes a stone Guanyin, in a shrine overlooking a lotus pond
with a 'face so beautiful it makes the lotuses shy to bloom'.
'At night, the shrine smells of ambergris.'

CURATOR....

LIM. I think we can make a quite educated hypothesis
that Baker took this statue / from the burning palace.

CURATOR. I'm sure the conservation team would be happy to review your research, but till then we mustn't –

LIM *flashes a whole series of facsimiles: yellowed records in handwritten Chinese, photographs of Baker in his soldier's uniform...*

LIM. 'S quite a / discovery, isn't it?

CURATOR. Quite a discovery.

LIM. The stolen treasures of the Old Summer Palace…
are scattered all over European museums…
And the Chinese badly want them back.

CURATOR. (*is completely deflated*) Yes.

LIM. Some context for you.
A statue can be an exile.
A refugee.
Like all refugees,
a witness to atrocity.
Men in shirt tails
Smoking cigars
Shaking hands
Agreeing to burn…
Burn, a palace
to the ground.
Let the men at it…
Let them rape the place…
Let them take what they want…
The chinks love their pots!
Break a couple.
Burn the rest.
Steal the prettier things.
The gold.
The marble.

CURATOR. Dr Lim.

LIM. Maybe a statue.

CURATOR. Amber[/Tony]

LIM. Or two.

3.

University office.

PROF, *white, and* STUDENT, *mainland Chinese, sit across a desk from each other.*

PROF. Again, it's perfectly within your rights *not* to go on the –

STUDENT. That is not

PROF. Not to… listen.
 Not to go, you and your friends,
 Perfectly within your right not to go /on the museum placement.

STUDENT. But…

PROF. But. Yes, then you'd fail the –

STUDENT. But it's a boycott, you can't just –

PROF. Listen. Given that the British Museum is *essential* to this –

STUDENT. You can't penalise us for –

PROF. It's a course about the Museological Experience.
 You understand that right?

STUDENT. Yes, but –

PROF. Honestly, it's…
 I mean why don't you channel this…
 emotion.
 Channel it productively?
 In life sometimes / you've got to…

STUDENT. We are. That's why we're protesting.

PROF. Sometimes you have to learn to sit with complex emotions, and –

STUDENT. Yuanmingyuan is a national humiliation
 for our country, you're not –

PROF. I understand it's a sore point.
I do, but –

STUDENT. You are not taking this seriously enough.

PROF. I am. Listen.
I'm listening, I'm empathetic.
These are... complicated issues.
But this is an administrative...
Obviously, you can't expect to
pass the course if you –

STUDENT. Then we will continue to –

PROF. No, please.
You can't.
You *can* but
these disruptions, / they're...

STUDENT. Protests.

PROF. Okay, sorry, protests.
It's not fair on the other –

STUDENT. The other students should also join us.

PROF. (*laughs*) Should they? Really?

–

STUDENT. It's hypocritical otherwise.
The way they talk in class about –

PROF. Okay, well.
Is the Chinese Student Society out there?
Calling for the return of...
of the Benin Bronzes?

–

Thought so.
You see, you can't be so selective. It's...

STUDENT. (*standing*)

PROF. What?

STUDENT. You are perpetuating white colonial / violence on...

PROF. No. No. *No I am not*.

STUDENT. Colonial / violence on Chinese students who want...

PROF. No, no, *no*. That is so clearly –
No!
Please.
Clearly I caught you out on... and you're just...

STUDENT. We only want to see accountability from...

PROF. (*shakes head*)

STUDENT. Please listen.

PROF....

STUDENT. We want to see you, the department, the university show us some solidarity.

PROF. Solidarity?

STUDENT. You mentioned Benin Bronzes.
Two years ago, you, the department...
You wrote an open letter to –

PROF. No, wait, listen –

STUDENT. And *you* signed it. You were –

PROF. I know, and –

STUDENT. We are simply wondering why you / and the department...

PROF. and I'm prepared to think about...

STUDENT. why today... in a very / similar situation...

PROF. about these matters...
They are *not* similar at all –

STUDENT. How come you show no solidarity with *our* cause.
And instead penalise us / for a legitimate...

PROF. Listen, these are *delicate* matters.

STUDENT. It is a simple demand.
   Please support our boycott of the British Museum.
   Until they engage in serious conversation
   with our government
   About the repatriation of –

PROF. Now these are *delicate*...
   They're complex. Nuanced. They need time to...
   But you're demanding, very loudly, unreasonably –

STUDENT. You are the one raising your –

PROF. No, I am being very civil, very –
   I'm being *very* reasonable...
   It's you lot who are out there *shouting* and *screaming* and *harassing*...!

   –

   Sorry.
   Harassing.
   Other students. And staff.
   Frankly, I feel very harassed by –
   Well, this conversation / but also...

STUDENT. Okay, I'm sorry if...

PROF. Okay, see that's a better start.

STUDENT. (*sits down*)
   I also want this to be...

PROF. Good.

STUDENT. Reasonable and –

PROF. So do I.

STUDENT. But, / I feel you're not...

PROF. And also. Sorry, let me...
   Thank you.
   Now, I'm empathetic. But *politically*...
   Politically, I... or rather
   Philosophically, I...

PART ONE 25

STUDENT....

PROF. I'm not sure I'm able to *align* myself with...
and that's well within *my* right!
Which of course you've not considered at –

STUDENT. I don't understand

PROF. You've not considered my rights to...
my right to... in *rejecting*...

STUDENT. The boycott.

PROF. Its *political* basis.

STUDENT. But this is not –

PROF. That is disingenuous.
You are well aware. Very well aware.
The college is very aware.
Of the Chinese Student Society and –

STUDENT. We do not have political links.

PROF. I am not saying that, I am saying there are definitely strong *sympathies* at play and –

STUDENT. But this is only –

PROF. No. *No*. I am *saying*, if you would listen?
Okay. I am saying that, you have *historically* shown support for...
or more accurately been *opposed to*...
opposed to other students advocating for...
very troubling issues like...

STUDENT. Like Hong Kong?

PROF. Yes. *Yes*, for example, Hong Kong. And –

STUDENT. So we cannot exercise our right to express our –

PROF. One hundred per cent you can, that is not in –

STUDENT. Or to counteract Western media bias?

PROF. By throwing eggs.

–

By *throwing* / eggs

STUDENT. I don't...

PROF. Throwing eggs at pro-democracy –

STUDENT. That was one person, one –

PROF. Who was at the time on the committee of –

STUDENT. Who is no longer a member of –

PROF. But the point remains that –

STUDENT. And he is not associated with this boycott.
Which is actually started by Chinese students
in *your* class, not by –

PROF. That doesn't change –

STUDENT. Actually this has very little to do with the Chinese
Student Society.

PROF. No, you're missing the...
entirely missing the...

STUDENT. You're not listening! We are your *students*...
Expressing our *discomfort* in...
(*stands up*)

PROF....
Can I speak honestly?

–

Can I speak honestly and can I trust that you will not misreport, or –

STUDENT....

–

PROF. Do I believe, broadly, in the return of stolen art?
Of course I do.

STUDENT. Then?

PROF. Am I also concerned about what your...
what the Chinese government...
More than concerned. Horrified.

I look at all this...
These protests in front of the museum?
These calls in the press for action?
I look at this and I think:
this is so clearly, so *obviously* a kind of,
public-relations campaign,
a distraction from –

STUDENT. But it –

PROF. No, listen. A distraction from...
Certainly from more pressing, more horrifying things.
political prisoners
disappearances
Muslim concentration camps.
Concentration camps!
And this new atrocity in Xinjiang.
Those dead people.
Fifty dead people.
Fifty *burnt* people.
Ten of them children.
Those people burning to death,
totally avoidable, / and, and...

STUDENT. And that has not happened in this country before?

–

PROF. That was deeply offensive.
Totally inappropriate.

STUDENT. That incident was a tragic accident.

PROF. The police started the fire.
They barred the doors.

STUDENT. We don't know that.

PROF. It was a peaceful protest.
They fired on...
Threw grenades into...

STUDENT....

PROF. And to look at all this, and to think that somehow
 returning a *statue*...
 that these are terms in which to think about *justice*?
 To give in to the idea of Chinese *victimhood* in this climate
 is...
 Absurd, frankly. It's absurd to me.

STUDENT....

–

PROF. I realise now this makes me very vulnerable to you.

STUDENT....

PROF. It makes me dangerously vulnerable to you.
 And I am afraid, honestly, I am. I am afraid of you.
 And what you could do, or say to me, about me.

–

–

STUDENT. Is it so hard to believe?
 That this matters a lot to us?
 It's... genuinely very upsetting.
 That... Please understand, this statue is not some...

PROF....

STUDENT. Not some political chess piece for us.
 It is...
 We are all living far away from family.

PROF....

STUDENT. And Guanyin is... a very maternal figure.

PROF....

STUDENT. We believe
 our parents believe she is watching over us.
 And we think about what the professor said
 in that video.
 About exile.
 About being far away.

And we understand that feeling.
Because we are so far away.
And we think of how this statue was...
About how long she has been away from home....
Taken away. From home.
For many of us it is an emotional...
A very emotional situation.

–

–

PROF. I didn't realise...

STUDENT. You know, we are capable of feeling things.

PROF. I didn't mean –

STUDENT. Many people in this university, in this country.
They do not try to hide how...
they think we are crass people.
Only care about money.
Gucci, Prada.
That everything we feel
we are somehow manipulated into feeling.
And maybe that is true?

Silence.

PROF. Are you afraid?
Afraid of...
Because I want you to feel safe in
This university
free, to question everything,
the ways
you might have been
manipulated, into feeling –

STUDENT....

PROF. to use your word

STUDENT....

PROF. not saying that you have, just...

STUDENT....

PROF. Sorry.

STUDENT. s'okay.

A bruised but tender silence.

When I first came to this university.
And stepped into your class, do you know?
What was the first thing you said to me?

PROF. When was –

STUDENT. You said: Juliette[/Julian]?
  Juliette[/Julian]
  That's a very interesting name.
  For someone like you.

PROF. I –

–

I meant...
I must've meant, I *mean*...
I'm *sorry*.
I hear now, how...
Obviously I meant...
I thought you would have a –

STUDENT. I do have a Chinese name

PROF. Okay.

STUDENT. But it vanished
  when I saw the relief.

PROF. Relief.

STUDENT. After you first laughed.
  At Juliette[/Julian], an interesting name
  for someone like me.

PROF. I –

STUDENT. After you laughed, then relief.

4.

Somewhere in the British Museum. Five very smart curator-types are having a crisis meeting. FOUR *is valiantly trying to convene the meeting;* ONE *and* TWO *are old hands;* THREE *is a feisty young department head;* FIVE *is taking notes.*

Outside, the sounds of a noisy protest occasionally bleed in, indistinct.

A noise from outside.

ONE. Jesus are they lighting firecrackers?

FOUR. Come on guys, thoughts, thoughts

TWO. Well the obvious problem with this wall-text business is that we'd then have to make new signs for / every bloody thing...

THREE. I don't think that's –

TWO. And what would it say, exactly?
    'This work of art was *allegedly* stolen'?
    'This work of art is currently under dispute'?
    'Look away if you can't deal with the fact that history
    / is a messy ugly thing'?

THREE. Come on that's so,
    we just want more criticality / in the display

TWO. And why now, why this object, why –

THREE. (*to* FOUR) It's never the right moment though!
    But now we have this opportunity,
    A real test to
    to decolonise the –

FOUR. Sorry to (interrupt) –
    upstairs need this end of day, so uh,
    that's pretty promising on the / wall text then?

TWO. Not to me, not that it matters.

FOUR. (*to* ONE) And you?

ONE. I dunno.
   I just think it opens us to more
   Blah blah blah on the Internet.

   Silence.

FOUR. (*to* FIVE) What about you?

ONE. She's not technically in this –

FOUR. Just, I can sense you've been wanting to say something.

FIVE. Oh.
   Didn't realise I could weigh in.

FOUR. No hierarchies here.

TWO. (*sotto*) We really gonna let the interns / run the museum now.

THREE. (*to* TWO) You're such a bully, do you know that?

FOUR. she's a junior curator.

TWO. I know! Was just a (joke) –

FOUR. I want to get some younger takes in the mix

TWO. No, no!
   You're just trying to force a consensus
   on all this woke posturing.
   Can I remind this group
   that a significant portion
   of our stakeholder base
   the public
   is very skeptical about
   these facile culture-war positions.
   Like those people, out there,
   demanding instant guillotine justice!
   's not our job to put
   this country
   or history, on trial,
   we're here to present the record
   from a position of
   practised
   academic
   / neutrality.

FOUR. Could you just let her,
/ (*to* FIVE) Go on, don't mind him

FIVE. Personally,
the wall-text idea,
it feels pretty pointless to me.

TWO. (*surprised beat*)

FOUR. Okay.

FIVE. (*pointing outside*)
I mean, those people are calling for return,
for total accountability.
Wall text just seems a bit –
dunno
Insincere and
/ museum-y
and performative

THREE. But this is a museum.   TWO. Okay great, can we move on?

FOUR. (*to* THREE) Come on,   FIVE. (*to* THREE) Sorry.
don't –

FOUR. No, go on.

FIVE. Well I suppose what I'm saying is,
is there a way we could,
in our response,
show more practices of,
of care?

ONE. Care, as in –   TWO. What does   THREE. That's
                        that even –   gorgeous.

FIVE (*pointing outside*). What people want
nowadays
need, rather,
is beating hearts and
conversation and
really getting into the muck of things.

and, I mean, the heart of this matter
this object
is
trauma, violence.

ONE. Well I rather think
the more interesting story is
the object's art historical –

FIVE. But now we know the Opium War is part of that
art historical journey.

–

ONE. 'S fair.
Yeah, 's fair.

TWO. Do we, though?
/ *Know* that, I mean, just...

THREE (*to* TWO). Jesus, did you even read / the report?

FOUR. Okay, okay.
(*to* FIVE) Just try'na drill into your...
so what, like a podcast?
Or expert panels or –

FIVE. Mm I don't –

THREE. I think the core of your idea is genuine engagement.

FIVE. Yes.

THREE. Which is fab, I mean that's our north star right there!
I think, on engagement, we should revisit my idea
about the special exhibition.

ONE. Think we all agreed   FOUR. No, no, no –
we'd put that –

THREE. The Story of Tea and Opium,
come on the synergy is (perfect),
there's plenty of maritime artefacts in the reserve collection
actual silver bullion, Canton dock ledgers...
and obviously the link to Hong Kong

is super on the pulse.
We like on the pulse!
(*to* FIVE) What do you...

FIVE. Well, yeah, but –

TWO. Oh my god.

ONE. Why are you always interrupting her?

TWO. Give me a break!
This is not our first rodeo.
It's incumbent on us
as always,
when faced with these spurious
anti-museum circuses,
to do absolutely nothing.
We do not feed the beast.
We do not / *engage*.

ONE. (*to* FIVE) Just finish your –

FIVE. What I'm trying to say is,
what's the version of events
where we,
I mean the museum,
relinquishes the voice of authority?
I mean, yes, we've gotta think about
protecting the museum
but do it in a way that's
dunno
bit less predictable and institution-y.
(*to* TWO) cuz doing nothing's not an option
not these days.
Sorry, it's just not.
And I think you know that.

TWO. Mm.

FIVE. Collectively you're some of the smartest
Most progressive
People in the field
I think you

we can do so much better
than a piece of wall text saying
'This statue was stolen and
we should've checked our receipts better.'
That's such low-hanging fruit.
We care so deeply about this work.
(*pointing outside*) Those people care.
They're our public too.
And they deserve better.

They turn to FOUR.

FOUR. Okay.

Silence.

So what do we do?

The group turn to FIVE.

FIVE. I suppose
How do we bring *people* together?
How do we transform the museum
into a space of *care*?
Like, how can we
literally *hold* space
For communities, you know, for
Grievance, for
for,

5.

Two Chinese lion dance puppets burst onto stage, accompanied by vigorous Chinese drummers.

They dance around the statue, dipping and diving.

The British Museum.

Projection: 'BRITISH MUSEUM LATES: CHINA X.'

Amidst the drumming, we hear, in voice-over, an exchange from a neighbouring panel discussion.

VOICE 1. We've got time for some questions.
Yes, lady in the purple jumper.

VOICE 2. Thank you, that was a lovely session.
'S a comment not a question.
All I have to say is if *we* hadn't gone in
well, it might have been the Germans.
Or the Japanese, down the line.
And I doubt they'd have been half as...
Well maybe the Japanese, I don't know, but certainly not the Germans.
And I know it's not very proper to say any of this but...

VOICE 1. This is a brave space, yeah, go ahead.

VOICE 2. I mean it's a beautiful statue and I'm glad it's still with us,
because, well, we only need to think, really
about, well, to be blunt,
The Cultural Revolution, don't we?

The drumming and lion-dancing continue.

Two Cross-Talk performers, A and B, British Chinese, appear in traditional costume.

A. Cross talk is the Chinese art of

B. Talking crossly (*hits a wooden block*)

A. No, don't interrupt

B. Don't be cross (*wood block*)

A. Could you –

B. Don't you cross talk me (*wood block*)

A. I'm just trying to explain to these nice people –

B. You'd better cross your t's, dot your i's then,
Or was that dot your t's and cross your eyes?

A. You're ruining everything!

B. Ah you're cross now

A. I am!

The lion dance tears through them.

A DRAG KING, British Chinese, appears, sitting on a chair, lifting weights.

DRAG KING. My Chinese Masculinity has always been this fragile, papery thing
These weights represent burdens of ancestors past
who maybe didn't have the words I do now.
Cuz in Chinese, the pronouns him and her sound the same.
It's a gift and a curse.
And so I lift for these ancestors.
I lift with them.

The lion dance tears through. Actually, maybe it's become a Dragon Dance, who fucking knows?

Again, we hear the neighbouring Q&A.

VOICE 2. I don't know why everyone here is getting so upset.
It's really no secret how you Chinese
eventually did much the same
to all your art
as the British did during the Opium War,
and if we hadn't collected so much of it, well...

The cross talk performers.

A. I am cross!

B. Why?

A. This is an important Chinese art form!
Older than Shakespeare, it is

B. So what? You're older that most folks 'ere.
Doesn't make you important.

A. You don't want to cross me

B. Thought that's the point

A. What?

B. Cross talk, innit? (*wood block*)

At the climax of this circus, POET *appears, British Chinese.*

The stage suddenly stills.

They perform a poem against a lo-fi hip hop version of Teresa Teng's《月亮代表我的心》*'The Moon Represents My Heart'.*

POET. We are
folding dumplings
in the shape of
paper boats,
me and Gran,
you are sitting on an altar
by the fridge,
and I ask Gran
if you are a man-god
or a woman-god
and Gran says
whatever you feel like

whatever you feel like

In this body of mine,
I feel lunar,
Just like you:
Ambiguous,
because the body,
like waves,
like gravity,
like sand,
can be a way
to chart celestial movements,
the passage in the sky of
heavenly bodies,
unconcerned with
just two ways of
knowing love.

TECH. (*off, on mic*) Yeah sorry that's time.

The lights shift. It was a sound-test.

POET. Was that okay?

TECH. Yeah, you happy with it?

POET. Suppose, yeah.

TECH. Sweet.

POET. Am I
　Do I –

But the TECH *has gone.*

The DRAG KING *enters.*

DRAG KING. Babes no way.

POET. (*seeing* DRAG KING) Oh my god!
　You're here for…?

DRAG KING. Yeah, yeah, you too?

POET. Nice. Yeah, just did a sound check.

DRAG KING. Look at us.
　Going places. Eh?

POET. Yeah, really cool.
　Did I miss your –

DRAG KING. Oh, I'm on again at nine, if you wanna…

Enter the two CROSS TALK PERFORMERS.

B. Ayyy!

A. Oh my god, babe!

B. 's like a lil reunion innit.

DRAG KING. Oh my god did they call you guys in too?

B. Yeah! Mate, you here to hang or…

DRAG KING. No, man, I was booked.

POET. He's on again at nine.

A. Sick, sick.

POET. What are the odds, eh?

DRAG KING. Yeah, didn't realise they knew so many of us.

Enter another ARTIST, *British Chinese.*

ARTIST. (*amidst a chorus of greetings*) No way!

POET. Under one roof.

ARTIST. What're you up to?

POET. Yeah, doing some spoken word.

ARTIST. The one 'bout your gran?

POET. Yeah, yeah.

ARTIST. Hey, sorry to hear she passed.

POET. Yeah no it was a while ago.

ARTIST. Me and the crew we're, uh, we're running this jiaozi-making workshop

POET. Jiaozi

ARTIST. Dumplings, mate, like Chinese gyoza

POET. Right, right.

ARTIST. Y'all should come.

DRAG KING. Yeah can't, I'm on again at nine.

ARTIST. We're uh, it's sorta like a,
we call it like a family circle?
we got some of our mums and grans…

A. Right, like a community uh, sort of –

ARTIST. Yeah, showing people how to…

B. Cool, cool.

ARTIST. fold dumplings, all the rest of it.

Long pause.

So uh.
Did y'all see the Lion Dance?

GROUP. Yeah, yeah.

ARTIST. They really pulled all the stops, eh?
So much culture, I could die.

Enter DJ, *British Chinese.*

DJ. Oh my god, what're you guys doing here?

The greetings are less exuberant now.

POET. Chinese New Year, apparently.

DJ. That's jokes.

POET. You uh

DJ. Spinning, yeah.

Long silence.

6.

A dance party in the museum. A group of hip YOUNG PEOPLE *dance to an electronic music remix of*《月亮代表我的心》 *'The Moon Represents My Heart'. They dance around the statue, variously moon ritual and bacchanal.*

7.

End of the night.

Lights on.

The room is empty. The floor is strewn with bits of trash.

POET, *same one as before, enters with a plastic bag. They approach the statue.*

POET. I guess I ought to
apologise.
About earlier. Cuz I
think I gave you fake dumplings.
I mean, in that poem?
About me and my gran and...

They weren't *fake*, they, I...
I've *made* dumplings before
obviously,
I have.

See it's this thing I have about dumplings,
like okay, I *make* dumplings
But it's this huge fucking
show of making dumplings
all the time.

I make and perform this
dumpling life and I wish
I *wish* so hard I could say and
not be wilfully misremembering
maybe even lying
definitely lying
that I'd made them with my gran?

Gran
whose funeral in Singapore
I missed
I skipped cuz
I had a show on
at Southbank.
Career-defining. Show.
Apparently I channelled the loss in my
performance.
They said it was transcendent.

And I guess in that way
even the gran in the poem is fake?

In reality she barely knew
my name or what to do with me.

Would freak out
about the whole
queer thing.
Let's be real.

I sell the fantasy, though,
of being that bitch
with the gran and the dumplings.

I've worn the cheongsam to the club
I've held the oriental fan
I've done the five stages of grief
with Uncle Roger.
Considered the diasporic
euphoria
of taking off my shoes
before going in...

I wish that apart from the outside of me,
which is clear to everyone,
that the inside of me could also
resist this tide of
saturated *whiteness* that
comes with breathing London air?

Most days I'm drowning in it,
and I want there to be
this chain, this
chain of people...
pulling me back
want it so...
so bad, this chain,
this chain
of my folks pulling me back
saying
no, no, no.
'Cept I don't know these people
won't know them
they are
darkness.

'fact they don't give a shit
about me.

Anyway.
I'm sorry that
I offered you fake dumplings.
Here in this hell you are in.

—

How are you?
Honestly?
How are you feeling?
Do you, like me, feel

this tide of
whiteness
watching you daily
you've been here so long
must do something to you.

Are you lonely?
You must be lonely.
Has anyone offered you
anything real lately?
Has anyone been
kind?

—

—

(*opens the plastic bag*)

Proper dumplings this time.
I got them from the Itsu next door but
I bet one-hundred per cent they're better than
the vegan ones I make?
I'm vegan, obviously.
I hope they help with
however you're feeling
And you don't have to
worry about me,

I'll be fine.
Thank you.
And sorry.
And...

(*bows weirdly*)

Thanks for listening.

POET *leaves the dumplings before the statue, awkwardly does a ritual gesture, and exits.*

8.

Across a desk in an office at the British Museum are MAN, *white British, and* WOMAN, *mainland Chinese, who speaks with an Americanised Chinese accent.*

MAN. Frankly the museum takes a strong stance against ethnic cleansing of the sort we've been hearing reports about, and...

WOMAN. (*retrieving a document*)
Okay.

MAN *gets up to show* WOMAN *out.*

MAN. I really don't think we've got
anything further to...
your employer, after all, is only a businessman.
Seeing as we've already spoken to high-level, very high-level
figures in your government and –

WOMAN. (*remains seated*)

(*places document on the table*)

–

MAN. This is?

WOMAN. Writ of gift.

MAN. (*reads it*)

–

This is.

(*counting the zeroes*)

And that's for.

WOMAN. Whatever you want to do with it.

MAN. From your...

WOMAN. Yes. He's only a businessman.
But he loves art.

MAN. Of course.
That does I suppose...
Change the
complexion...
Of our conversation.

WOMAN. We understand that the central heating is...

MAN. The heating...

WOMAN. Is a bit leaky.
So we'd like to help
with the central heating.

MAN. (*laughs*)

WOMAN. And of course, we would
strongly encourage

MAN. Encourage

WOMAN. Strongly *hope* that
you will reconsider
the request of the Chinese Ministry of Culture and Tourism.

–

MAN. Thing is, we don't *sell* art, Ms Zhang.

WOMAN. This isn't sale. It's facilitation.

MAN. Right.

WOMAN. Sale is when, for example,
my boss, they call him Chinese Indiana Jones,
when he went to the house of
that French fashion designer,
Yves Saint Laurent?
And he paid Mr YSL in cash three times what
he had paid at auction
for the bronze Zodiac heads
stolen from Yuanmingyuan
The Rabbit and the Rat,
which were formerly on a fountain,
an architectural centrepiece.

MAN. Yes.

WOMAN. See, in *that* case, with Mr YSL,
honestly I think it's a much more vulgar case.
For a museum to hold stolen art is one thing.
For an individual…

MAN. Yes.

WOMAN. Mr YSL, when my boss first started going after him,
he apparently moved the Rabbit and the Rat
next to the toilet.
He said 'they were fountain heads after all'.
At the time he had some strong political views
about Tibet.

MAN. …

WOMAN. But he took the money anyway.

–

MAN. Uh.
Listen, Ms Zhang.
It's very, very unlikely.
That we can…
Do as your employer hopes.
It's a legal matter you see, there's

WOMAN. The British Museum Act, / I know

MAN. So then you know.
   Our board of trustees…
   Their hands are tied.
   I mean it's…
   Not *pretty* but it's a finicky law.
   What we *could* arrange…
   Maybe a loan? Of some sort.

WOMAN….

MAN. Perhaps a long-term loan.
   Essentially repatriation.

WOMAN….

MAN. Repatriation in everything but name.
   We could work with a Chinese museum to house it.
   Yes, we could facilitate a whole process.
   We could certainly arrange for something like that.

WOMAN….

MAN. It's worked very well with, for example
   Nigeria and the –

WOMAN. We are not Nigeria.

   –

MAN. No. You're not. But –

WOMAN. And you would take the money all the same.

MAN. The heating does need work.

WOMAN….

MAN. We could arrange for numerous items.
   Numerous items of great interest to –

WOMAN. Your board of trustees.

MAN. Yes.

WOMAN. If I were to say, for example
   that Mr Declan Taylor?
   His multi-million-pound

>   ten-hectare
>   residential development
>   At Nine Elms?
>   If construction were
>   suddenly, to be massively delayed.
>   Because De Yi Shipping
>   which runs his supply of
>   high-density concrete between Middle East and
>   Europe, were to cancel some contracts.
>   For example, if I said,
>   My boss is on the board of trustees.
>   Of De Yi Shipping?

MAN....

WOMAN. Also, Lord Francis Cooper
> has substantial financial interests
> in a new tech park at
> Canary Wharf?
> The campus was recently acquired
> by a Chinese real-estate developer
> whose CEO's son
> went to Cornell with
> my boss.

MAN. I don't know what to do with this information.

WOMAN. They play *Overwatch* together.
> I heard.
>
> –
>
> I think you misunderstand.
> This meeting is not a request.
> This is a courtesy call.

MAN....

WOMAN. Because anyway the repatriation order has to come from you.

MAN. (*pointing to document*) And this

WOMAN. Personal touch.
   Guan xi, as you all like to say.
   Although I notice you've not even offered me coffee.

   –

   It's really quite cold in here.

MAN. I'm sorry. I could –

WOMAN. Please.

   He gets up.

   Goes to a Nespresso machine.

   Starts making her a coffee.

   While it brews:

MAN. If I may ask
   what is your employer's real interest in all of this?

WOMAN. Patriotism.

MAN. Oh really.
   As simple as that.

   The coffee brews.

WOMAN. Did you know that
   When they burnt down Yuanmingyuan,
   They found three hundred servants
   Burnt to death in the wreckage?

MAN....

WOMAN. When my boss
   When he got the Zodiac heads
   back from Yves Saint Laurent
   there was a ceremony.
   At the New Chinese Museum.
   Those decapitated heads,
   finally returned to China
   after a hundred and sixty years.
   Makes me think of *The Odyssey*.

You know, when Achilles
returns the body of Hector?
Something sacred about return
That makes people weep.
Priam wept. Achilles wept.
All of Greece and Sparta wept.
Something sacred about return
even when you have to pay
millions of euros.
(*points to table*) Or pounds.
In China, maybe we're old fashioned
but we still respond to these things.
Imagine, after one hundred and sixty years,
after three hundred burnt bodies,
a century and a half of national humiliation,
at the end of the day
to care so much about
a rabbit's head, a rat's head...
(*shakes her head*)
Life is very funny, isn't it?
They livestreamed the ceremony, you see,
to classrooms all over China.
I was a student then.
When we saw...
I'm talking seven to twelve-years-old
children
when we saw this ceremony,
we, children, we wept.

–

That feeling alone...

He brings her the coffee.

She looks at it, packs her things, and stands up.

I mean let's put it this way.
When you finally return our Guanyin to us,
Who will have died to move it?
Who in Britain will miss it?
And who in Britain will weep?

9.

CLEANER, *holding a hoover is cleaning the area before the statue.*

CLEANER *stops. He looks at the statue, as if he hears something.*

Nothing.

He resumes his hoovering.

He stops to gaze at the statue.

He draws closer.

He watches and watches the statue. A shiver in the space, perhaps the faint glitter of spirits, watching.

CLEANER *is very emotional. Perhaps he cries.*

He says:

CLEANER. 's that…
   Did you?

   An aching silence, as if something might reply,

   Then,

   A team of CONSERVATORS *crashes into the scene – it's a rush of rubber gloves, calipers, clipboards, and a very large wooden packing crate.* CONSERVATOR *supervises.* CLEANER *watches for a while, then exits.*

CONSERVATOR. Statue of the Bodhisattva Guanyin in Royal Ease
   Chinese make
   Song Dynasty, twelfth century
   Place of Origin, China

   Two spectres appear. It is the YOUNG SOLDIER *and* YOUNG WOMAN, *from before. She is clinging to his leg, gnawing it.*

Enter WITCH ONE, *from before, who sees the two spirits. Over the following exchange:*

The team wraps the statue.
They lift the statue.
They fasten the statue in the box.
They drill braces into the box.

WITCH ONE. (*to the* YOUNG WOMAN) Are you hurt?

YOUNG WOMAN. Yes. It burns.

WITCH ONE. Where?

YOUNG WOMAN. Everywhere.

WITCH ONE. Why don't you just leave?

YOUNG WOMAN. Can't.

WITCH ONE. Why?

YOUNG WOMAN. I'm angry.

WITCH ONE. Why?

YOUNG WOMAN. He saw me.
  Foreign devil.
  He saw me hiding
  He saw me, our eyes
  Locked, he saw
  He knew we
  Were there
  And still he...

CONSERVATOR. Gift to the Museum, collection of CT Loo, 1917.
  Weight, fifty-two kilograms
  Last conservation exercise, 1998

WITCH ONE. But if you hug the fire
  like that...
  Wouldn't it be easier to let go?

YOUNG WOMAN. No.

CONSERVATOR. Material, carved white stone
   Remarks, comparatively rare material for this make.
   Appearance, traces of paint, discoloured
   minor salt bloom, damage to the surface layer

WITCH ONE. No?

YOUNG WOMAN. He'll escape.

WITCH ONE. Escape?
   Where would he go?

YOUNG WOMAN. I don't know.
   Home.

WITCH ONE. I think this is the end of the road for him.

YOUNG WOMAN. What?

WITCH ONE. It's the oldest magic.
   Build a house,
   and someone will live in it.
   His people,
   they've built this temple to
   to hold the worst,
   darkest parts of themselves.

YOUNG WOMAN. What do you mean?

WITCH ONE. This is his hell, not yours.

CONSERVATOR. considerable staining from fire damage
   hairline cracks in the surface layer
   minor chipping on the bodice

YOUNG WOMAN. I've been in hell?

WITCH ONE. Yes, and don't you miss
   sky? And grass, and sun,
   and insects, and
   mud and rivers
   and stars
   and cool nights?
   They miss you.

YOUNG WOMAN *releases the* YOUNG SOLDIER, *who falls on the ground, muttering.*

See?

WITCH ONE *takes her hand.*

Not so hard, after all.

YOUNG WOMAN. What is he saying?

WITCH ONE. Never mind.
That is between him
and himself.
And you?

YOUNG WOMAN. I feel wind.
On my skin.

YOUNG WOMAN *turns into a bird and flies away.*

The team fasten the lid onto the box. They drill it shut.

CONSERVATOR. Condition, acceptable.

WITCH ONE *looks long and hard at the* YOUNG SOLDIER, *then exits.*

The YOUNG SOLDIER *remains, alone, muttering.*

YOUNG SOLDIER. This, this, this
is a part of me I
never knew I had.
This is a part of me
I didn't grow up
knowing.
This part of me
is not the hills of
Scotland not
the quiet hollow way
the woods where I stole a kiss
from my girl before I left…
this is not the part of me that's
long summer days and
dirt paths, not the deer
eating blackberry leaves

is not the deer's soft head
is not simple manners,
is not Ma telling me
you reap what you plant
so plant good things
gentle things
this is the part of me that
isn't good or gentle
isn't bonny
isn't milk and bread
around the fire
isn't cheese at breakfast
isn't biscuits
isn't stories
isn't songs
isn't kisses
isn't...
this is a part of me
I didn't know I had
but it was always
had been has
been there because
how easy it was to
do as I was told,
how easy it was
thinking on those
savage chinks
to take torch and sword,
this part of me
came right out of me
like cumming past
a point of no return
going
burn, burn, burn,
BURN IT ALL DOWN.

Slowly, other muttering figures, all men, all white, appear near him. A tableau of muttering ghosts, displayed on stage like exhibits.

This is the part of me
that pressed down
on the throat
of the part of me that
drank in
the Chinese mountains
thought how pretty
the hills
the quiet forest glade
the palace gardens
the blue moon
the part of me that
saw a deer running
across a quiet brook
and thought
deer in the East
are like deer in the North
and thought of
blackberry leaves
thought of Ma slicing
cheese and
thick bread and…
how good the world
could be
but no,
no,
this is the part of me
that stayed
held by some power
King and Lord
knowing too late
'twas something
Satanic
in the sergeant
barking
fuck your ma
fuck your goodly
soft insides

fuck your girl
fuck the chinks

—

So this is the
part of me
that lingers
far beyond the
natural life of a
feeling.
This is the part of me
that stains my good name
my ma's good name
the part of me that
that took aim at men's guts
thinking of their mothers' eyes
lit gunpowder
thinking of the sound
of bones snapping
burnt things down
burnt the other parts
burnt the goodly
soft parts of me down
burnt things
in the name
of freedom
(*laughs*)
Freedom
now, here,
I know,
I can never be
free.

Finally, the statue is removed from the space, perhaps hoisted away.

End of Part One.

PART TWO: THE PEOPLE'S REPUBLIC OF CHINA

1.

A white interrogation room. Hong Kong.

MAN, *Hong Kong Chinese, is sitting in a chair.*

WOMAN, *mainland Chinese, has just put a bun on the table.*

There's an open folder between them, which WOMAN *occasionally writes in.*

WOMAN. (*points at the bun*)
　Eat.
　No?
　(*Tears it in half.*)
　(*Smells it.*)
　You take half, I take half.
　Share the calories.
　You scared of getting fat?
　(*laughs*)
　(*eats*)
　It's not too bad.
　Bit dry.

　(*Goes to* MAN, *takes the bun, holds it to* MAN*'s face.*)

　You have to eat.

MAN....

WOMAN. (*sighs*) No, you have to eat.
　If not you might say we didn't feed you.

MAN....

WOMAN. Mm?

MAN....

WOMAN. You won't complain?
Do I have your word?

MAN. (*nods head*)

WOMAN. You sure?

MAN. (*nods head*)

WOMAN. (*eats the second half*)

–

What are you thinking?

MAN. Nothing.

WOMAN. You're thinking about going home.

MAN. Yes, I've been here for –

WOMAN. Tell me, is this what you expected?
I mean, you guys...
When you do these sorts of things
at the back of your mind
surely you're mentally prepared to
be called in.
I'm curious, like, what do you people
expect?
Did you expect more people?
Did you expect there to be dogs?
Did you expect there to be food?

MAN. I want to go home.

WOMAN. Yah, I know, we've been through that.
That's why I'm asking.
Did you really expect that
you could come here
not cooperate
not give us anything
and then go home?
And you didn't even eat the bun.
Someone bought that specially you know?

>   Because you are a famous artist,
>   you know?
>   That's not very nice.

MAN. I'm just a cartoonist.

WOMAN. Okay.

MAN. I'm a cartoonist.
>   I just draw what's on my mind.

WOMAN. Okay.

MAN. I just draw what's on my mind.
>   There's nothing more to it.
>   I don't even know why I've been –

WOMAN. You don't know?
>   Then why did you use an encrypted server?
>   To upload this image?
>   Why use an anonymous profile?

MAN. ...

WOMAN. (*writes this down*)
>   Cuz clearly for us there's an issue here.

MAN. I don't know about / any issues.

WOMAN. cuz certain iconography –
>   You understand what I'm saying?
>   Iconography?
>
>   Iconography.

MAN. Yes.

WOMAN. Certain iconography
>   Is now problematic.
>   You understand? You can't just draw
>   umbrellas, for example

MAN. I (didn't) –

WOMAN. Not saying you did,
>   just explaining that –

MAN....

WOMAN. Certain iconography
   Like handcuffs.
   Which you *did* draw –

MAN. They're not handcuffs.

   –

   They're ropes.

   –

WOMAN. Ropes.

   Ropes?

MAN. Ropes, around her wrists.
   Ropes. You have a problem with ropes?

WOMAN. Not really, no –

MAN. She's often drawn with ropes.

WOMAN. Really?

MAN. Yes. It's one of her... accessories.
   Like the lotus.

WOMAN....?

MAN. If she's portrayed with ropes, it means something

WOMAN. Means what?

MAN. Means in this form, she ties up evil.

WOMAN. Ties up evil.
   Okay.

MAN. Yes.

   –

WOMAN. Like what?
   What is evil?

MAN. Anything.

WOMAN. Anything. Like?

MAN. Bad people.

WOMAN. Bad people, okay.
And in the current context?

MAN. What current context

WOMAN. In the current context,
would you say that...
No. *Who*
do you consider
bad people to be?

–

MAN. I don't know.

WOMAN. Rapists?

MAN. Maybe.

WOMAN. Thieves?

MAN. Maybe.

WOMAN. Homosexuals?

–

MAN. What?

WOMAN. Are you a homosexual?

MAN. How is that –

WOMAN. I'm just curious.
Are you a homosexual?

–

MAN. I've made my statement.
The ropes around her wrists symbolise
the binding of evil.

WOMAN. Okay, thank you.
Would you say the ropes are about...
Justice, for example?

MAN. I don't know / what you mean.

WOMAN. Justice for your friends?
For your boyfriend?

–

MAN. No.

WOMAN. I understand they were
arrested recently.
For demonstrating.
About the Uighurs.
So are the bad people...
the police?

MAN. No.

WOMAN. Are the bad people
the government?

MAN. No.

WOMAN. Am I a bad person?

MAN....

WOMAN. (*laughs*)
Okay, good progress.
Anyway. Look.
It's clearly not rope,
please don't...

(*laughs*)

You want to tell me, of all people,
what a handcuff is or isn't?

MAN. I...

WOMAN. I was saying.
Certain iconography, is now
deemed sensitive.
The minute I see handcuffs?
I have to act.
And here, we've got handcuffs

around the wrists of Guanyin?
That's very odd.
To me.
Maybe you can explain.

MAN. That's not Guanyin.

WOMAN. (*laughs*)
Okay humour me, who is it?

MAN. My mother.

Silence.

WOMAN. Okay.
Let's not waste more time.
Listen, shall I just tell you
my interpretation of your cartoon?
And then you can just say yes
Or no.
If I'm wrong, and I'm very
prepared to be wrong,
You can go home.
Okay?

MAN....

WOMAN. A reminder, you are being recorded.
Your reactions are being recorded.

MAN....

WOMAN. Now.
What I think
is.
The cartoon, which shows the Guanyin in handcuffs –

MAN. I object to that characterisation –

WOMAN. The Guanyin in handcuffs
is you playing / on the idea of

MAN. No, no, you're not / listening to me

WOMAN. The Guanyin being extradited to China.

MAN. What?

WOMAN. Extradited.
 Forcefully returned.
 Now can you see how that
 opens up a can of worms?
 Because extradition is
 also a sensitive idea nowadays.
 Can you understand?

MAN....

WOMAN. And you know, we can read it a few ways.
 That is the great thing about your cartoon.
 Honestly, I really admire it.
 It's very, very clever.
 The art style is raw, but the
 concept.
 I chuckled when I saw it.

MAN....

WOMAN. Did you know I studied drawing in school?
 I admire you, you know, I…
 I mean that, genuinely.
 Anyway.
 Clearly, you also think the statue?
 Should have remained in Britain.

MAN. What!

WOMAN. No?

MAN. That is *not* at all –

WOMAN. But it's a totally legitimate interpretation.
 And given our current circumstances,
 yet another can of worms.

MAN. What circumstances?

WOMAN. Public order.
 Counter-terrorism.

MAN. Peaceful demonstrations are not terrorism.
 Genocide is terrorism.

She notes that down. He winces.

WOMAN. You saying the statue should remain in Britain
is suspiciously close to saying
that *Hong Kong* should also remain –

MAN. No that is *not* –

WOMAN. And, you know, in the current context
all this is also very sensitive.
Are you a separatist?

MAN. No!

WOMAN. Then why are have you drawn a separatist cartoon?

MAN. I haven't.

WOMAN. Then why does the Guanyin look so miserable?

MAN. What?

WOMAN. I mean, her *face* is just so...

MAN. I don't know.

WOMAN. Why isn't she happy to return to China?

MAN. I don't know.

WOMAN. Wouldn't you be happy if you could go home now?

MAN....

WOMAN. Do you support the protests in Britain?

MAN. No.

WOMAN. (*slides a photo*)
Then why have they printed your cartoon on their T-shirts?

MAN. I can't control what –

WOMAN. Do you have Western allegiances?

MAN. I don't, I –

WOMAN. You studied in London, didn't you?

MAN. Yes, but

WOMAN. Have you used your Western networks
to fuel hostile sentiments abroad?

MAN. I did not make the cartoon for –

WOMAN. Who has put the Guanyin in handcuffs?

MAN. I don't – she's not in handcuffs, she's –

WOMAN. Is it the government?

MAN. I've told you, / they're not handcuffs

WOMAN. Are you implying that the government is tyrannical?

MAN. What? No, it's –

WOMAN. A police state?

MAN. No.

–

WOMAN. It's all there. It's plain for us to see.
Your cartoon promotes separatist ideas.

MAN. It does not.

WOMAN. Your cartoon promotes anti-China sentiments
abroad.

MAN. It does not.

WOMAN. Your cartoon portrays the government
as violent and tyrannical

MAN. It does not.

WOMAN. Your cartoon is critical of
the police

MAN. It is not!

WOMAN. Please don't insult my intelligence.
I have a great deal of respect for you
as an artist.
We all do.
But please don't think
that things like metaphor are lost on me.

–

MAN. You cannot pin down metaphor.

WOMAN. Oh?

MAN. You cannot pin down meaning.

WOMAN. Okay.
So tell me, what have you drawn?
If it is none of the things I've said?

MAN....

WOMAN. Nothing?

MAN....

WOMAN. Okay, so –

MAN. You are wrong.

–

WOMAN. Okay, good.
So tell me, what am I seeing?
What am I not seeing?

–

–

You said it was your mother.

(*laughs*)

MAN. It is my mother.

WOMAN....

MAN. She is preparing rope

WOMAN....

MAN. So she can hang herself

–

Her life is evil.

WOMAN....

MAN. Because her heart is broken

–

Because she has raised a son
Who is only good for drawing cartoons
And that is not enough at all.
He's wasted his life.

–

Her heart is broken
because she has raised a son
Whose future is to suffer.
Because she lied to him
When he was growing up.
Saying there was a future
Other than suffering.

–

And you're wrong
The look on my mother's face
is not sad at all
Not even angry.

WOMAN....

MAN. It is joy.
   Do you understand?
   Joy?

WOMAN....

MAN. Because when she hangs herself
   she will be free
   from the cycle of history
   of moving from one fire to another
   one tyranny to another.
   she will be in a place where
   all the best possible futures
   all the best unborn futures
   converge like many rivers
   into an ocean as deep and wide
   as the universe
   and she will spend eternity
   exploring them on a ship

and it is as if
the present were only
one pathetic
drop
in that ocean.
They are forgetting waters.
And she won't even remember
what had broken her heart in the first place.
And no one there will remember,
because all of this will pass away
like it did before.
That is the meaning of my cartoon.

—

—

Can I ask you a question?

WOMAN....

MAN. Do you really want to live in this world?
Where mothers hang themselves from grief?
Would your mother be proud of you today?

WOMAN....

MAN....

WOMAN. Is that your statement?

MAN. (*nods*)

—

—

WOMAN. Okay.
Interview over.

    WOMAN *exits*.

2.

Beijing. A party in a luxury apartment.

The statue is on display here inside a glass case.

MAN *and* YOUNG MAN, *both Chinese, are chatting while* WOMAN, *white, listens on.*

Unless indicated, MAN *and* YOUNG MAN *are speaking in Mandarin. So does* WOMAN, *but in simple, memorised phrases of Mandarin. We hear this in English.*

YOUNG MAN. I'm not much into art

   (*pointing to the statue*)

   I mean, I don't really know about these things
   I'm just a straightforward guy…

MAN. No, don't say that about yourself.

YOUNG MAN. I can't wrap my head around these things, you know?
   History. Ancient history, things like that?
   But wow, what you said about correcting history, I mean…

   (*mindblown*)

WOMAN. (*laughs*)

MAN. No, no, it's nothing.

YOUNG MAN. No, no, no, please.

MAN. Least I could do.
   I mean all that matters is that it's all come full circle.

YOUNG MAN. Yeah?

MAN. Yeah.

YOUNG MAN. Cheers, cheers, cheers.

MAN. Cheers.

WOMAN. Cheers!

   They toast.

YOUNG MAN. I mean, it's very inspiring to me.
Your story. We are both from the same town.

MAN. Yes, yes, yes, your accent.

YOUNG MAN. I've driven past your old neighbourhood it's...

MAN....

YOUNG MAN. Oh sorry, I mean

MAN. It's a slum.

(laughs)

YOUNG MAN. *(laughs)*

WOMAN. *(laughs)*

YOUNG MAN. Yes, yes, yes.
And now you... well now you are so well-respected that even the Culture Minister, wow...

MAN. No, no, no, we are old friends.

YOUNG MAN. I mean, still.
I can't believe he really just let you keep her!
Just in your / house, like that.

MAN. No, no, no, it's only for a few weeks.

YOUNG MAN. I mean, still!

MAN. I did put a lot of money into...

YOUNG MAN. Of course, of course, of course.
Just so amazed.
And by the way, this is such a great party.
Your house is...
Just amazing.
Congratulations again.
Cheers, cheers, cheers.

WOMAN. Cheers!

MAN. Cheers.

They toast.

So who do you know here?

PART TWO   75

YOUNG MAN. My boss, over there, is Wang Lei.

MAN. Oh, yes, he and I are...

YOUNG MAN. Old friends, I know.

MAN. You work for his firm?

YOUNG MAN. Risk management, yes.
  Deputy Head.

MAN. Ah, good for you,
  good for you.
  You're quite young, too.

YOUNG MAN. Yes.

MAN. Very impressive.

YOUNG MAN. Thank you.

  (*pleased beat*)

  So after this, where is she

MAN. The Guanyin?

YOUNG MAN. Yes, where is she going?

MAN. Pudong Airport.

YOUNG MAN. Oh! On the way to
  The Palace Museum or...

MAN. No. She stops at Pudong Airport.
  They're installing her there.
  It was my suggestion.
  The Ministry liked it.
  The whole world passes through Shanghai, you see.
  And I thought, who goes to a museum?
  What use is a museum?
  Things like her deserve something bigger, you know?
  The message is clearer in a place like
  Pudong Airport.

YOUNG MAN. Of course, of course, of course.

MAN. What do you think the message is?

YOUNG MAN. Ah?

MAN. The message.
As a young Chinese,
what do you think it is?

–

YOUNG MAN. Culture.

MAN. Maybe.

YOUNG MAN. History.
Justice?

MAN. Strength.

YOUNG MAN. Ah.

MAN. She's beautiful, isn't she?

YOUNG MAN. Honestly, I thought she would be bigger. She's like a small child.

MAN. (*big laugh*)
I like your honesty.

YOUNG MAN. Actually I did wonder. Knowing these white people

MAN. (*laughs*)

WOMAN. (*laughs*)

YOUNG MAN. What if they just returned a copy?

MAN. A copy?

YOUNG MAN. A replica. Kept the real one for themselves?

MAN. Oh that wouldn't matter.

YOUNG MAN. Ah?

MAN. Yeah, it wouldn't.
It's not the art that matters.
It's the story around it.

>   They could've kept the original
>   For all I care.
>   It'd basically be an old rock.

YOUNG MAN. I see. I see.

MAN. You're paying for the story, you see.
>   And the story around it? Is that
>   the Chinese Government
>   with a little bit of help from a patriot,
>   managed to get it back
>   for the price of central heating.
>   Well more than that, but you get the idea.
>   The story around it is that they
>   were strong once,
>   which is how they took things from us
>   And now that they're on the way out?
>   We take things from them.
>   That's a story worth paying for.

YOUNG MAN. I see. I see.

MAN. All of human history? It's basically
>   people taking things from each other.

YOUNG MAN. I should be writing this down.
>   Pearls of wisdom.

>   (*laughs*)

MAN. No, no, no.
>   Just, the truth.
>   Only the truth.

YOUNG MAN. Man, I'm standing here with a real hero.

MAN. No, no, no.

YOUNG MAN. Listen, uh, sorry if this is...
>   If this is inappropriate,
>   I know we are at a social thing...

MAN. No, no

YOUNG MAN. I uh, obviously, I idolise you.
And it's my life's dream to work for you some day.
Really.

MAN. Ah.

YOUNG MAN. And obviously I hope that some day is...
Sooner than later.

MAN. (*laughs*)
That's okay, work and pleasure are
all the same to me.
And I'm always interested
to see how I can help,
especially young people,
especially from my hometown.
What would you like to discuss?

YOUNG MAN. Wow.
Wow, wow, wow, uh.

—

Is it okay if I...
Go to the bathroom to freshen up?
I want to have a proper conversation,
and I'm just a bit...

MAN. No, please, please.

YOUNG MAN. (*shaking his head in disbelief*)
Thank you. Thank you.
I'll be back, very soon.

MAN. Take your time.

WOMAN. (*makes to go with* YOUNG MAN)

MAN. (*to* WOMAN, *speaking in English*)
No please stay,
we can practise my English.

WOMAN. Oh!

MAN. (*to* YOUNG MAN) Go, go.

YOUNG MAN. I won't be long.

YOUNG MAN *exits*.

MAN *speaks fluent English with a slight Chinese accent.*
WOMAN *speaks with a thick Arkansas accent.*

WOMAN. Oh my lord. You speak

MAN. Yeah, course.

WOMAN. (*laughs*) Oh my lord, I'm sorry
I'm just, spilling all my wine here.
You speak English! How cool is that?

MAN. I spent many years in the States.
So the two of you are colleagues?

WOMAN. Oh right, no,
we um, we're just friends.

MAN. Friends. I see.
How do you know –

WOMAN. Oh from, just, from being around.

MAN. Your accent…

WOMAN. Oh I'm from Arkansas.
Originally.

MAN. Arkansas.

WOMAN. I know, crazy right?
I mean, it's pretty wild.
Just last month…

(*shakes head*)

Uh, where'd you spend time in the States?

MAN. I went to Cornell.

WOMAN. Cornell. That uh, that's in

MAN. New York.

WOMAN. I see, yeah! The college, that's right.
Oh that's crazy.
Yeah, yeah, uh
that's amazing.
And now you're uh
You work in uh…
I mean, obviously, this is *your* house which is uh
Pretty fucking amazing, if you ask me.
Pardon the uh – I mean, this is
this is the biggest house I've ever been in.
I'm pretty sure, I saw a swimming pool?
in one of the other rooms?

(*laughs*)

I mean

(*mindblown*)

MAN. So, what brought you here?

WOMAN. *Here* here? Oh, um, well I came with –

MAN. No, I mean, to China.
To Beijing.

WOMAN. Oh, to *China*.
Well uh, in short? Work.

MAN. Work. Yeah, as in…

WOMAN. Oh I uh, mainly I just uh
I wouldn't call it work, I uh
I hang out, you know?
I uh, I'm a bit of a social butterfly?
I uh, go to lotsa parties, like this one?
I mean, it's only been a month, really?

MAN. Oh you're a party girl, then.

WOMAN. Yeah! Yeah, you get it!
Oh, you're so nice.
I mean, I've met lotsa rich people here,
not all of 'em speak English, so it's uh,

breath of fresh air.
I uh. I'm a little homesick,
Truth be told, I uh,
it's only been a month really.

MAN. So what were you up to before...

WOMAN. I was uh, I used to work in um, entertainment.

MAN. Oh, like acting, or...

WOMAN. No, no, nothing like...
I dealt blackjack in Atlantic City.
So not too far from where you were.
And uh, well, I got
approached one day cuz
one thing I will say about myself?
I've got a winning personality.
And one day, someone came up to me n'said:
Hey, you should come work in China.
And uh, well, here I am!

MAN. I see.

WOMAN. Now, you're nice, so I don't mind
telling you: at first I thought,
oh my lord, is this gonna be some sorta
like an *escort* thing, but uh

MAN. Right.

WOMAN. Yeah, no, turns out it's uh, really just
turning up. Standing around.
Looking happy. Laughing.
I uh, you know sometimes they just
pay us to stand around at events and
drink wine. And I do love wine.
I've done a couple of weddings,
some... I think they were like
business-type things.
And uh, things like this.
It's a pretty wild... pretty crazy uh
gig.

Fun, that's for sure, and the
money's pretty good.
Oh but I'm just talking your ear off.
'fact I think I might've said too much.
(*points to drink*) This wine is strong.
We're not usually meant to uh
say too much. Discretion, you know, and uh
I guess he's, he's… a client
more than a friend, but uh
today he's my friend, if you get my…

MAN. Yeah, no I get it.

WOMAN. But uh,
Hey, if you don't tell… I won't!

MAN. You're fine.

    YOUNG MAN *returns*.

WOMAN. Aw, you're a sweetheart.
And uh, he's coming back.
Hey!

They switch back to Mandarin.

YOUNG MAN. I think someone was doing cocaine inside the –

MAN. Why have you brought this low-class woman into my house?

–

YOUNG MAN. What?

MAN. Your whore.

–

YOUNG MAN. She's uh.
She's not a whore.
She's my colleague.

MAN. Do you really think so lowly of me?

YOUNG MAN. Of course not.

PART TWO 83

MAN. That you think you've got to bring some
idiot white woman to my house?

YOUNG MAN. No, no, no

MAN. To impress me to –

YOUNG MAN. No, I'm sorry if –

MAN. To make yourself seem more...
What? Tell me.

–

YOUNG MAN. I don't know. It's just...
I wanted to make a good impression.
I wanted to...

–

MAN. Take her and get out.

YOUNG MAN. No, please, it's a misunderstanding.

MAN. Don't make a scene.

WOMAN. (*in English*) Is everything okay?

MAN. (*in English*) All good.

YOUNG MAN. Sir. Please.
Let me just...

Long pause.

The thing is.
I wasn't lucky enough to...
I didn't manage to go overseas.
And nowadays, you know how
it's important for people to be...
To have that sort of...
To be exposed.
I'm just... following the trends.
I'm sure you understand.
I hope I didn't make a bad impression.
I'm sorry.

Maybe I'm still quite
provincial after all.
I only went to a normal university,
but, you see, obviously I
managed to work hard
and get into
a good company
and climb up and
so I think that shows...
I have a good attitude, / and a...

MAN. You have a shit fucking attitude.

YOUNG MAN....

MAN. Listen. I like you.
But you need to learn.
I didn't spend millions on getting this
fucking statue back from the West
only for young Chinese to feel
like they need do shit like this.
To parade this white clown around
Thinking it makes you look more
high class.
Sickening, frankly.
Why is this impressive?
How does this reflect well on you?
The only thing I see reflected
is the same
pathetic
old world habits
old world mental traps
old world beliefs.
She's a dumb hick.
She's nothing.
She's literally worthless.

YOUNG MAN. I understand.

MAN. Do you?

YOUNG MAN. I do.

MAN. See, I don't need this kind of
shitty
insecure
white cocksucking
attitude in my company.
That's not how I became who I am.
That's not who I want around me.
Are you going to fuck her?

YOUNG MAN. What?

MAN. Are you going to / fuck her

YOUNG. No, that's not the –

MAN. So you don't understand.
Listen.
You need to think of her
like, I dunno, an accessory.
like a Prada bag. Worse.
Worth less.
Prada bags you can collect.
I wouldn't want this one
in my house any longer than
it takes to cum inside and
throw her out.
You understand?

–

YOUNG MAN. I think so.

MAN. You asked to talk,
so I want you
to learn something today.
Only because we are from the same hometown.
And it makes me sad to see you
think so lowly of yourself.

YOUNG MAN. I'm sorry.

MAN. Say sorry to yourself, not me.

YOUNG MAN. I understand.

MAN. Listen.
>You can pick any room in the house.
>Otherwise, we don't have anything to talk about.
>And I'll have to have some serious words
>with my friend Wang Lei over there,
>about his risk-management deputy
>who has, in my opinion, some
>severe cultural deficiencies.
>
>–

YOUNG MAN. I don't think that's...
>Something I can...
>I actually have a girlfriend.
>...
>
>Okay? I don't... really
>Plus, she's not a (prostitute)

MAN. ...

YOUNG MAN. ...

MAN. (*makes to leave*)

YOUNG MAN. No, no, no Sir.

WOMAN. (*in English*) Did I do something wrong?

MAN. (*in English*) No, not at all.
>It was lovely to meet you.

WOMAN. (*in English*) Oh *likewise*.
>You have a good one, now.

YOUNG MAN. Sir.

MAN. (*in English*) Good night.

>(*exits*)

YOUNG MAN. ...

WOMAN. (*laughs*)

3.

Pudong Airport, Shanghai.

The statue is on display in a busy corridor, inside a glass case.

Nearby, MAN *and* FRIEND, *mainland Chinese, are sitting near a boarding gate.* MAN *is very nervous.*

FRIEND. It's a nice boat
 High-class boat.

MAN. Really

FRIEND. Nice boat from Amsterdam
 Almost like a mini cruise
 Almost a ship

MAN. Wow, really.

FRIEND. There's a bar.

MAN. A bar, wow.

FRIEND. Open bar.

MAN. Meaning

FRIEND. Drink as much as…
 Drink your worries away.
 (*laughs*) You'll need to because
 Soon you'll be working so hard.

MAN. Yes. Okay.

FRIEND. Don't worry.
 Trust me.
 I've done this so many times.

MAN. Okay.
 I'm just

 —

FRIEND. You said you were ready.

MAN. Huh?

FRIEND. For an opportunity

MAN. I know

FRIEND. I told you to be ready

MAN. I know, I know
It's just
only this morning I was...
only this morning
And now

FRIEND. They'll understand

MAN. I just, I
don't want them to

FRIEND. You can call them when you reach

MAN. Will I be able to get a SIM card there?

FRIEND. Of course.

MAN. What kind of SIM card?
British number or

FRIEND. British number, obviously.

MAN. They might not...
They won't know it's me they
They might not pick up.

FRIEND. They'll be surprised.
That's all.

MAN. Oh.

FRIEND. It'll be fine.

MAN. Why did you have to take my phone?

FRIEND. For your safety.
For my safety too.
Listen, the fewer people who know...

MAN. I understand, but they're family.
They're not 'people'.

FRIEND. They'll understand.
   You're doing this for them.
   You know that right?

MAN. Obviously.

FRIEND. Don't forget.
   Think of the mansions.
   The big houses.

MAN. I know.

FRIEND. Just six years and you can

MAN. Six years…

FRIEND. You can order one house
   One for each of your family

MAN.…

FRIEND. Look at the one,
   The one our old classmate built
   you were always so envious.

MAN. I know.

FRIEND. So beautiful, right?
   His house.
   Looks like a mansion from Venice

MAN. Yes

FRIEND. He only did five years you know?
   He worked very hard.

MAN. Yes.

FRIEND. Two thousand pounds a month.

MAN. One pound is…

FRIEND. Eight.
   Lucky number.
   Eight times what you earn
   driving trucks.
   Extend your life by eight times.

Retire eight times earlier.
Your wife, she can have
eight times of all the bags she wants.

–

What's your concern?

MAN. The boat, it's...

FRIEND. The boat is safe.

MAN. No, but the boat, it's...
I've heard that –

FRIEND. Don't listen to –

MAN. I've heard that –

FRIEND. Those are other companies.
Other companies who
cheat your money and

MAN. I'm just going by what I've heard.

FRIEND. They don't plan it properly
they don't have the right logistics
so they go at the wrong time
they don't use secure channels
they're stupid, see, they...
it's not that easy to get caught

–

MAN. Get caught by

FRIEND. By fishermen, sometimes they're
busybodies, these fishermen
who see and they

MAN. Not police?

FRIEND. No, not police, never police

MAN. Fishermen.
But why do fishermen come with guns and

FRIEND. Guns? Where are you hearing

MAN. I read, in the news.
Last year.

FRIEND. Don't believe everything you read.

MAN. I know, but it said there were guns and dogs
it said

FRIEND. Listen, this is my job.
I've been there.
Who would you rather listen to?
Me or those newspapers?
It's an exaggeration
To discourage people from...

MAN. Five men drowned, they said.

FRIEND. Not that many.

MAN. What?

FRIEND. Only one drowned.

MAN. Oh, why?

FRIEND. He got confused.
Didn't listen to instructions.

MAN. But the other four...

FRIEND. They weren't Chinese.
Vietnamese. So.

–

–

MAN. I'm going to pee.

FRIEND. No.

MAN. Why?

FRIEND. You'll run.

–

MAN. Run?

FRIEND. I know.
 I've seen this before.
 It's normal.
 Breathe, please.

MAN. Okay.

 (*breathes*)

 (*he gets up*)

FRIEND....

MAN. I just think it's too fast.

FRIEND. I know, it's very fast.

MAN. Why is it so fast?
 Why can't I have a few days?

FRIEND. It's logistics, I told you already.

MAN. There's no other boats?

FRIEND. There's only one boat.

MAN. Okay, but
 Maybe, just give me my phone I'll

FRIEND. She'll make you think twice

MAN. She won't, she

FRIEND. They always will, I've seen it before

MAN. Just want her to know

 Boarding announcement.

FRIEND....

MAN. Please. Please.

FRIEND. Okay fine.
 Very quick.
 No details.
 If not deal's off, you're on your

MAN. I won't.

FRIEND. (*hands him phone*)

MAN. (*dials*)

  (*long ring*)

  –

  No one's.

FRIEND. (*to himself*) Shit.

MAN. No one's...

FRIEND....

MAN. Hello?

  (*long pause*)

  Listen, I.
  No I'm... I know. It's...
  Listen!
  I had to go.
  I have to go.
  I have something urgent
  Uh. Personal.
  Far away.
  Yah. I'll tell you more next time.
  Very soon, call you when...
  I get there.

  There.
  Holiday. I –
  Holiday.

  (*long pause*)

  Yes.
  No.

  (*long pause*)

  I've got to go.
  I'd better not.
  No don't, just
  Tell her I...
  Tell her I...

FRIEND. Faster.

MAN. I've got to go.

   (*Hangs up*)

   FRIEND *snatches phone*.

   MAN *is very shaken. He's emotional*.

FRIEND. I shouldn't have

MAN....

FRIEND. See, this is why.

MAN. I'm fine.
My mum.
Shit.
Can I call –

FRIEND. No.

MAN. She's old, she's –

FRIEND. Where is the man
I spoke to this morning?
You were so excited!

MAN. I was

FRIEND. I said it's time and you
dropped everything
stopped your work
you didn't even want to
shower the dirt off your –

MAN. I wasn't thinking

FRIEND. You *were* thinking you
were thinking of

MAN. I wasn't thinking properly

FRIEND. Stop it!

   –

   If you change your mind

PART TWO   95

MAN. I've changed my mind, yes
　　I've changed –

FRIEND. I cannot give you anything –

MAN. What, / but we haven't even –

FRIEND. I cannot give you anything back.

MAN. We haven't even taken off.

FRIEND. No, it's done, it's paid.

–

MAN. But half my savings, just
　　You said deposit, you said

FRIEND. I told you.
　　To be sure. To be ready.

MAN. But, that's

FRIEND. I told you.

MAN. But

FRIEND. I told you.

–

　　Listen, it's done.
　　It's done.
　　You're okay.

　　This is normal.
　　You miss them.
　　You have regrets.
　　But you'll regret it more not going.
　　I know.
　　So many of us have made the trip.
　　So much success.
　　So much money.
　　Your family will thank you.
　　They're with you, they're with you.
　　(*touches chest*) Here. Okay?

This is the hardest
decision you'll ever make.

MAN. It is…
I don't want to…

FRIEND. It's the most
important decision
you'll ever make.

MAN. I'm sorry.

FRIEND. Please.

MAN. I don't know.

FRIEND. (*holds* MAN)

(*long silence*)

—

(*seeing the statue*)

Look over there.
You're blessed.

MAN. Blessed?

FRIEND. See who has come to bless
Your journey?
Maybe you should…

MAN. Should

FRIEND. Pray.

MAN. Pray.

FRIEND. Would that make you feel…?

MAN. Yes.

FRIEND. Okay. Then.

They go to the statue.

Boarding announcement.

Make it short and sweet.
Okay?

PART TWO 97

MAN. I uh…

FRIEND. Hurry.

MAN. Please keep my family safe
Please keep my mother safe
Please keep me safe

FRIEND. Very good.

MAN. Please bless my journey
Please bless the wind
Please bless the water
Please don't let the water…
Please don't let the fishermen…
Please don't let the…
And when I get there
Please bless my hands
Make them hard-working hands
Please bless my heart
Make my heart…

Boarding announcement.

Make my heart strong.
Like stone.
Like you.

FRIEND. Come on.

MAN. Please, make me like stone
That can float on water.

FRIEND. Come on.

MAN. Okay.

FRIEND. Let's go.

MAN….

FRIEND. Let's go.

> MAN *hesitates.*
> *Makes to go.*
> *Makes to go.*
> *Makes to go.*

4.

The same airport. Another day.

The same spot. The statue gazes down at a row of seats where a YOUNG MAN, *Uighur, sits. A* YOUNG WOMAN *lies sleeping on his shoulder. They're both sopping wet.*

An older MAN, *mainland Chinese, stands near the* YOUNG MAN.

MAN. (*checks watch*) 's been two hours.

YOUNG MAN. Has it?

   (*checks his phone*)
   (*chuckles*)

   Probably missed my flight.

MAN. Where to?

YOUNG MAN. Morocco.

MAN. Really.

YOUNG MAN. Missed it.
   Don't ask me why Morocco

MAN. Why Morocco

YOUNG MAN. I wanted to see the spice markets

MAN. Oh
   We have spice markets here in Shanghai.

YOUNG MAN. I know but –
   You're so unromantic.
   So typical.
   Typical Chinese.
   Aren't you ever curious?
   About those olden times?
   When we were all
   One big continent?
   Not like today, cut up like beancurd.

MAN. Sure.

YOUNG MAN. Camels.
Horses.
Caravans.
Y'know near where I live –
used to live, before...
I used to live in a town not too far
From the edge of the desert.
It's said there are still wild horses there
descended from the ones who got away
from the caravans. The Silk Road.

MAN. Really.

YOUNG MAN. Yeah, they have rust-brown coats.
My grandma, she used to say,
probably because of all the cinnamon...

(*laughs nervously*)

Do you like cumin in your food?
You're not a Northerner.

MAN. No.

YOUNG MAN. 's all the rage now.
In Rotterdam.
's where I live.
'nway.

MAN. Morocco.

YOUNG MAN. As a boy, I used to think
how far did those traders use to go?
Through the hills
The desert...
Morocco's about the fingertips of one arm from us,
if you spread your arms out wide...

The YOUNG MAN *demonstrates, spreading his arms wide.*

The MAN *flinches.*

As a boy I used to dream of Morocco.

The YOUNG MAN *shifts his body, the* YOUNG WOMAN *slumps into his lap, she's not sleeping, she's drugged, or catatonic. The* MAN *tenses.*

MAN. Listen,
is she…

YOUNG MAN. Don't worry she's fine.

MAN. Can I…

Motions towards YOUNG MAN.

YOUNG MAN *readjusts* YOUNG WOMAN *so she's slumped on his shoulder again.*

YOUNG MAN. She's fine.

MAN. Sorry.
Did you…
What did you…

YOUNG MAN. It's just ketamine.

MAN. Okay.

YOUNG MAN. Back away.

MAN. Okay.

YOUNG MAN *turns behind to look at the statue.*

YOUNG MAN. It came from India, actually.

MAN. What?

YOUNG MAN. (you stupid?)
The Guanyin.
It's been all over the news.
Or haven't you been…
Big victory over the whites.
Blah blah blah.
I'm not very patriotic.
cuz anyway, if you go back long enough?
India.
Not the statue, I mean, Guanyin herself.

Come on we all know this.
Journey to the West?
Everything's from India.
Everything's from somewhere else.
Nowadays everyone likes to pretend otherwise.
Get so worked up about it.
'Are you really from here?
Why don't you look Chinese, sound Chinese?
Are you Chinese?'
What's Chinese, even?
You and me, what makes us Chinese?
You know, I'm a Muslim.

MAN. Is that what you're after?
The statue?

YOUNG MAN. Mm.
I've heard her calling in my sleep.

MAN. Really.
What does she say to you?

YOUNG MAN. I want to die.
She says to me.

MAN....

YOUNG MAN. I'm not crazy,
I can tell you think I'm crazy.
Hard not to look at this poor fucking thing
torn about like a piece of meat
between two feral dogs
And not feel a little twinge of sympathy.
Don't you think our government
Is a bit like a dog foaming at the mouth?
Fucking slobbering thing.
Smallest thing will set it off.
Will rip the face off a baby if it came to it.
Tell me something,
why do you work for them?

MAN. Work for...

YOUNG MAN. (*points upstairs*)

MAN. Just a job.
Listen, don't think about that now.
Tell me about Morocco.

—

—

YOUNG MAN. Can you ask them?

MAN. Who?

YOUNG MAN. Them.
Whoever's whispering in your ear.
Can you ask them?
Ask them,
Why those people had to die?
And die in that way?
Burnt alive.
Couldn't the police hear them?
Screaming in the house as it...
Why did the police fire bullets into the street?
Why were there grenades and bombs
When all the people were carrying were
pieces of paper
and cooking pots?

MAN. I...

YOUNG MAN. And can you ask them?
I'm being serious.
Ask them.
Where is my brother?
And my second cousin?
And my uncle, his dad?

—

—

Can you ask them?
I mean it, can you ask?
I haven't seen them in...

MAN. I don't

YOUNG MAN. Not in five years.

MAN. I can ask.
Sure.
Would you then
Would you...

YOUNG MAN. To be honest
I think they're...
They're probably...
We accepted that,
Me and Mum.
When we fled to Rotterdam.
What do you think?

MAN....

YOUNG MAN. See when she comes to me in my dreams
Guanyin,
and says
I want to die
I wonder if there were nights
They woke up
My brother, and cousin, and uncle
Woke up in whatever
Shithole...
And thought the same.
I want to die.

MAN. Listen, stay calm.
But you know I'm right.
Whatever happens,
you've already fucked it up
for a lot of people.
Your people.
You realise that, right?
You've crossed a line.
Whatever happens
Whether I
Or she

Or you
Get out of this alive
You've already *fucked* a whole...
They? They're already drawing a web
that connects everyone you've ever known
'n tomorrow they'll net them all in the night.
You know this.

YOUNG MAN....

MAN. It's a matter of degrees now.
If you ask me.
If you cooperate
Show yourself to be
Calm
Reasonable...
At worst, temporarily insane.
Then it might not be so bad.
Might unfuck it a little bit.
If no one is hurt.

YOUNG MAN....

MAN motions closer.

MAN. Now, all I want to do is (*motioning closer*)

YOUNG MAN. Don't touch me.

MAN. Just let me take her to –

The YOUNG MAN *pulls back.*

The YOUNG WOMAN *stirs.*

Shit.

She wakes up.

Looks up, dazed, confused.

She stares at YOUNG MAN.

YOUNG WOMAN. What's happening?
Who are you?
Let go, my neck hurts.

MAN. Miss, I need you to stay calm.

YOUNG WOMAN. What's happening?

MAN. Miss you're safe, okay?
No sudden movements, please.
The police are watching out for you.

Red lasers train on YOUNG MAN*'s chest.*

The situation dawns on YOUNG WOMAN.

She starts to hyperventilate.

She starts to whimper, cry.

She starts to struggle.

Miss, please don't aggravate him.

YOUNG MAN *pulls himself and* YOUNG WOMAN *up onto their feet.*

YOUNG MAN. (*to* YOUNG WOMAN) Come on, time to get up.

YOUNG WOMAN. Oh my god please don't hurt me.

In YOUNG MAN*'s right hand is a lighter or torch.*

Moments pass in silence, then:

MAN. No, give me more time, please.

YOUNG MAN. What?

Suddenly, armed POLICE *close in. They surround* YOUNG MAN, *training their guns at him.*

POLICE. Okay this is over.
Let her go.
We have a clear shot.
We will shoot.

Long silence.

The YOUNG MAN *drags the* YOUNG WOMAN *over to the statue, he holds her in front of him as a shield. She wails.*

YOUNG MAN. The newspapers said
all China rejoices
because this statue has been returned to us.
All China rejoices
because historical injustice has been redressed.
Okay, I say fuck all China!
fuck all of you who looked away
while they
burnt our homes
dragged us from our beds
shot at us in the streets.
They want us to disappear
from the face of the earth.
Fuck all of you.
Fuck this statue.
Who fucking cares.
I want them back
Who'll return them to me?
My uncle.
My cousin.
My brother.
Hundreds of us.
Thousands.

MAN. We'll take you to them.
We'll find them.
You and me, together, we'll

YOUNG MAN. Will you show me their bodies?
Will you return their bones?
Will you tell them it'll be okay?
Will you tell them?
That we'll be free one day?
If not here,
then on the other side,
and over there will be
hills
and desert plains
and horses
and wind!

Tell them
Tell everyone
the mad dog will be shot in the eye
Its jaws will fall from our ankle
The regime will fall!
The king's eyes will turn milky
The king will die
His palaces will rot and then
burn
his armies starve and defect
the horses in his cavalry
burst from their stables
run back to the wild plains again
kick up the sand in a great storming
stampede, screaming into the wind
crush the mad dog's skull underfoot

The YOUNG MAN *breaks the glass around the statue.*

A shrill alarm goes off.

The YOUNG WOMAN *screams.*

YOUNG WOMAN. Please please please please please

POLICE. Let her go!

YOUNG MAN. we will crush the running dogs underfoot!
all of us who have been bound
and buried
will one day run wild and rebellious
across the toll-gates
and borders
and walls
that keep us imprisoned
one horse for every
man and woman
child!

POLICE. Let her go and no one will be hurt!

YOUNG MAN. The regime will fall!
The regime will burn!

YOUNG MAN *lets* YOUNG WOMAN *go, she screams and runs away.*

The YOUNG MAN *sets himself on fire.*

He wraps his arms around the statue.

He and the statue are engulfed in flames.

The regime will fall!
The regime will burn!

POLICE. FIRE
　　FIRE
　　FIRE

They fire on the YOUNG MAN.

They fire on the statue.

Both are shot to pieces.

Smoke. Fire.

A pile of stone on a bloody plinth, riddled with bullet holes. Then:

5.

The seaside. Waves. Wind. Gulls.

Two figures emerge from the darkness, ancient.

A STONEMASON, *chipping at a rockface, pulling stone, and loading it into a basket.*

A MOTHER, *sitting, on the edge of the cliff, enjoying the breeze, sitting in 'Royal Ease'.*

Her head in one hand, a baby in the other arm.

STONEMASON. The stone's so soft.

MOTHER. Mm.

STONEMASON. Easy to cut.

MOTHER. What's that?

STONEMASON. Nothing.

Several moments pass like this, in quiet repose.

Behind them, spirits linger in the darkness, watching.

The sound of the pickaxe against stone.

The baby gurgles awake.

The STONEMASON *gathers his basket of stones. Hauls it over to the* WOMAN. *He kisses her forehead. She smiles at him.*

The baby coos.

WOMAN. Oh, shh.
 Yes.
 Yes.
 I love you too.

The spirits leap into the air, become birds and horses. They fly away.

End.

A Nick Hern Book

Scenes from a Repatriation first published in Great Britain as a paperback original in 2025 by Nick Hern Books Limited, The Glasshouse, 49a Goldhawk Road, London W12 8QP, in association with Royal Court Theatre

Scenes from a Repatriation copyright © 2025 Joel Tan

Joel Tan has asserted his right to be identified as the author of this work

Cover design by Guy Sanders at Keeper Studio

Designed and typeset by Nick Hern Books, London
Printed in Great Britain by Mimeo Ltd, Huntingdon, Cambridgeshire PE29 6XX

A CIP catalogue record for this book is available from the British Library

ISBN 978 1 83904 424 3

CAUTION All rights whatsoever in this play are strictly reserved. Requests to reproduce the text in whole or in part should be addressed to the publisher.

Amateur Performing Rights Applications for performance, including readings and excerpts, by amateurs in the English language should be addressed to the Performing Rights Department, Nick Hern Books, The Glasshouse, 49a Goldhawk Road, London W12 8QP, *tel* +44 (0)20 8749 4953, *email* rights@nickhernbooks.co.uk, except as follows:

Australia: ORiGiN Theatrical, *tel* +61 (2) 8514 5201,
email enquiries@originmusic.com.au, *web* www.origintheatrical.com.au

New Zealand: Play Bureau, 20 Rua Street, Mangapapa, Gisborne 4010,
tel +64 21 258 3998, *email* info@playbureau.com

United States and Canada: Casarotto Ramsay and Associates Ltd, see details below

Professional Performing Rights Applications for performance by professionals in any medium and in any language throughout the world should be addressed to Casarotto Ramsay and Associates Ltd,
email rights@casarotto.co.uk, www.casarotto.co.uk

No performance of any kind may be given unless a licence has been obtained. Applications should be made before rehearsals begin. Publication of this play does not necessarily indicate its availability for performance.

www.nickhernbooks.co.uk/environmental-policy

Nick Hern Books' authorised representative in the EU is
Easy Access System Europe – Mustamäe tee 50, 10621 Tallinn, Estonia
email gpsr.requests@easproject.com

www.nickhernbooks.co.uk

@nickhernbooks